SouthernFried

SouthernFried

More than 150 recipes for crab cakes, fried chicken, hush puppies, and more

JAMES VILLAS
Photography by Jason Wyche

HOUGHTON MIFFLIN HARCOURT
Boston · New York · 2013

Photography copyright © 2013 by Jason Wyche

Cover image by Jason Wyche

Interior design by Elizabeth Van Itallie

Food styling by Mariana Velasquez

Prop styling by Martha Bernabe

Published by Houghton Mifflin Harcourt Publishing Company, New York, New York

Published simultaneously in Canada.

www.hmhbooks.com

Library of Congress Cataloging-in-Publication Data

Villas, James.

Southern fried / James Villas; photography by Jason Wyche.

 p. cm.

Includes index.

  ISBN 978-1-118-13076-6 (cloth); 978-0-544-18824-2 (ebk)

  1. Frying. 2. Cooking, American—Southern style. 3. Cooking—Southern states. I. Wyche, Jason. II. Title.

TX689.V55 2013

641.5975—dc23

2012040262

Printed in China

SZN 10   9   8   7   6   5   4   3   2   1

To Linda and Bruce Weed

Contents

Preface

Sizzling, Crisp, and Delectable

In a nation where organicized, locovorized, artisanized, and molecularized foods are now aerated, sous-vided, nitro-poached, tweezered, and prepared in every other trendy, offbeat, outlandish, and often geeky way imaginable, let's hear a general big round of applause for those familiar, traditional, beloved ones that are still being simply . . . fried. And since nowhere in this country can fried food boast the same cardinal role it plays in home kitchens and restaurants throughout the South, I say it's high time that special attention finally be focused on golden clam fritters, honey-battered fried chicken, crumbed pigs' ears, okra beignets, rice croquettes, blistered goobers, venison burgers, hot water cornbread, peach turnovers, and dozens of other wonderful deep- and shallow-fried specialties that contribute so much to the proud Southern table.

I'll also be so bold as to say that only Southerners fully appreciate and truly understand the fine art of frying, the instinct and obsession being in our blood since the days as youngsters we were taught to batter our first pieces of chicken, heat our first skillet of lard or shortening for a batch of fried green tomatoes, and carefully lower our first basket of plump oysters into a pot of sizzling fat. Gradually we learned that frying is a process whereby hot fat coaxes moisture from the interior of foods (creating the bubbles that rise from the fat) while browning the exterior evenly; eventually we came to understand that the ideal to aim for is surfaces that are crisp without being greasy and interiors that remain tender and succulent; and perhaps the biggest lesson of all was that when fried food is executed sensibly and calmly, no style of cooking is easier, quicker, and more fun and gratifying for cooks, family, and friends alike.

Myself, I was born, bred, and weaned on fried foods in North Carolina, and today my enthusiasm is as strong as when my mother would fry thick, sapid slices of aged country ham with red-eye gravy for breakfast, or when I'd get an initial whiff of crusty catfish at river fish fries, or when another bowl of piping-hot hush puppies was served with a brace of glistening quail in the Carolina Lowcountry. Southerners might not know a lot about grilling, steaming, sautéing, or even stir-frying, but when it comes to cooking foods in any form of hot fat, passions are intense, convictions are rigid, and judgments can be brutal. We may be gracious and modest about most matters, but if there's a serious Dixie cook who doesn't have definitive pronouncements on what constitutes good and bad fried chicken, shrimp, pork chops, onion rings, cheese grits, johnnycakes, and half-moon fruit pies ("light as a cloud," "crisp but moist," "lip-smacking flavor," "soggy as a dishrag," "greasy and disgusting," "dry and tough as whitleather"), I've yet to meet such a person.

As for other Americans, what astounds me today is how so many, ridden with guilt, have been conditioned by health and nutrition zealots to spurn and even fear the very fried foods they love to eat most—and make no mistake that, despite feigned denials, there's nothing we relish and crave more than well-fried chicken, potatoes, onions, sandwiches, and doughnuts. Folks are led to believe that all fried foods are automatically messy and dangerous to prepare, heavy and greasy, difficult to digest, packed full of dreaded calories and cholesterol, and generally a disaster. Hogwash. It is true that many of the dishes made with inferior ingredients and carelessly fried in old, stale fat at mediocre restaurants around the country can be pretty lousy, and nobody denounces the atrocities more than Southerners accustomed to better fare. It's equally true that frying is a cooking process that requires the right equipment, attention to certain sensible safeguards, and a willingness to make mistakes before the techniques are fully mastered. But it's also true that, since fried food is best within minutes of being removed from the bubbling fat, nothing lends itself more to the convenience, ease, and casual atmosphere of the home kitchen, and that once you've become hooked on the procedure, you'll grasp why Southerners have always championed fried foods over all others.

While there can be no doubt that the dishes celebrated in this book constitute a large percentage of the Southern diet, nothing is more misguided than the common perception that Southerners nourish themselves exclusively on fried foods without concern for moderation, nutritional values, calorie counts, and overall well-being. Just the basic information in the book's Introduction (which I encourage you strongly to review) should serve to prove that Southern cooks approach every aspect of frying very seriously and intelligently, and that we have little patience with those who might blindly condemn a style of cooking that, when handled with a bit of know-how and lots of common sense and respect, is altogether as disciplined, sophisticated, refined, and, indeed, healthy as any other. We Southerners view these dishes as the ultimate comfort foods, and we enjoy nothing more than sharing them with those who love and appreciate great eating. It's my bet that once you get the hang of frying, perfect your own ideas and strategies, and gather a few equally eager souls in the kitchen and around the dinner table, you'll derive the same relaxed joy and satisfaction from the exciting experience as any Reb does.

Introduction: Frying Basics

Equipment

Electric Automatic Deep Fryers. Available in all major stores under familiar brand names (Cuisinart, Calphalon, Hamilton Beach, Presto, Waring, and so on). Most modern-day countertop electric fryers boast such up-to-date sophisticated features as lockable lids, heavy wire mesh baskets with cool-touch handles, digital thermostats and timers, special filters to reduce odors, viewing windows, removable parts for easy cleaning, indicator lights or audible alarms for overheating, and even detachable magnetic cords for added safety. Storage can be a problem with models that are not compact, but today nothing is more reliable, easy to use, and safe than a sturdy single- or dual-basket deep fryer that can accommodate up to a gallon of oil and 2 pounds of food and is intended mainly for items that need to be immersed in at least 2 inches of hot fat. I have a compact dual-basket fryer that I find fully adequate for such smaller foods as oysters and shrimp, zucchini strips and onion rings, French fries, hush puppies, fruit turnovers, and the like. Prices vary dramatically from about $50 up to $300, depending on the size, style, quality of metal, and special features.

Dutch Ovens and Cast-Iron Pots. Ideal for deep-frying (with minimum spattering) larger foods like chicken, quail, small whole fish, jumbo shrimp and crawfish, and certain croquettes and fritters that require plenty of oil or other fat. While heavy-gauge Dutch ovens (preferably enameled) and cast-iron pots may not have the convenience and safety features of electric deep fryers, they are standard equipment in many Southern kitchens where lots of deep frying is done. When shopping, look for 7- to 8-quart vessels about 5 inches deep that have flared sides and domed covers. Some come with sturdy wire baskets that fit neatly inside and have long, open handles possibly with an extra groove for attaching the basket to the rim of the pan for easy draining of foods. The best of these vessels are made of cast iron or black steel, both of which distribute heat evenly and keep the fat at a steady temperature.

Skillets (Frying Pans). Without question, the most popular and important all-purpose equipment for both deep and shallow frying of all sorts of foods that do not necessarily need to be fully immersed in hot fat. The finest skillets are those made of heavy metals

that transmit and maintain heat evenly, and nothing beats either cast-iron or stainless steel pans with thick aluminum disks that cover the entire bottom and assure even cooking without hot spots. Most of the skillets used in this book are large in diameter (10 to 12 inches) and at least 3 inches deep, but serious Southern cooks pride themselves on nothing more than a collection of different-sized pans (I have eight cast irons, some inherited from my mother and grandmother) for different types and quantities of fried foods. Stainless steel and enameled cast-iron skillets are expensive but can provide years of successful frying if properly cared for. Rugged, moderately priced regular cast-iron pans last a lifetime and, to maintain their smooth surfaces, need only to be "seasoned" from time to time by lightly coating all surfaces with vegetable oil or shortening and "baking" the pan for about an hour in a 350°F oven. (One of the best investments is a deep, 10½-inch, 3-quart Lodge cast-iron "chicken fryer," which is perfect for frying all sorts of foods.) As for nonstick skillets, including those made of heavy cast aluminum, I do not recommend them for frying since the surface coating cuts down on the heat that reaches the food and there's high probability that anything you fry will be soggy and never develop the crispy surface characteristics of nicely fried foods. Frankly, I don't prefer nonsticks even for frying eggs, making grilled cheese sandwiches, or cooking omelettes.

Electric Frypans. My North Carolina mother swore by her stainless steel electric frypan for frying chicken, and, truly, nobody produced better Southern fried chicken than my mother. Once the rage in most American kitchens, electric frypans do have their merits (a steady heat, convenience when stovetop space is limited, detachable heat controls that make the pans dishwasher safe, and moderate prices), and I might well use my stainless one for various fried seafood puffs, fish strips, popcorn crawfish, vegetable fritters, and yes, even fried chicken. Yet no electric fryer will ever replace a conventional cast-iron or stainless skillet since the electrics heat up and cool too slowly, they can't be shaken to move food around, and typically high wattage means you can easily burn food if not watched very carefully.

Heavy Saucepans. Relatively small (2-quart), heavy-gauge stainless steel or aluminum saucepans come in handy for frying small quantities of shrimp and oysters, seafood and vegetable fritters, sausage balls, and beignets without wasting lots of cooking fat. Saucepans are also necessary for prepping some ingredients to be fried and for preparing certain batters and coatings.

Frying Baskets. All electric deep fryers and some cast-iron and black steel frying pots and bowls come equipped with wire baskets intended to lower foods into hot fat and drain them after frying, but if a basket is not included with a vessel, I urge you to buy one separately to facilitate deep frying—especially small items like shrimp and oysters, meat nuggets, cut okra, and hush puppies. The best baskets are made of a chrome-and-nickel combo and have handles that are placed high and stay cool during the frying process, but any sturdy metal basket that fits into a pot will do.

Deep-Fat Thermometers. Since the success of any frying involves preheating the cooking fat and maintaining it at the proper temperature, a good deep-fat thermometer of sturdy construction and with very clear temperature markings and a clip that holds safely to the side of the pan is essential. Choose either a glass-tube thermometer fastened to a flat, long stainless steel frame with a metal clip on the back, and/or simply a smaller glass thermometer with easy-to-view temperature markings and a sliding clip on the back. The first is ideal for deep frying with large quantities of fat, and the second for lesser amounts.

Slotted Spoons, Spiders, and Tongs. It should be taken for granted throughout this book that, whether directed specifically or not in a recipe, foods fried in 1 or more inches of oil or other fat that need to be turned for even browning should be turned with either a metal slotted spoon, wire mesh spider, or sturdy set of metal tongs, depending on the size of the food. No matter what I'm frying in whatever amount of fat, I always have these handy tools close at hand for all types of possible needs.

Splatter Guards. Any way you look at it, frying can be messy and possibly dangerous, and to reduce the amount of sizzling fat splashing on stovetops and unprotected hands and arms, nothing is handier than a wire mesh splatter guard with a looped handle that sits on top of a vessel while food is frying. Companies like Le Creuset make expensive guards in lightweight enameled steel, but even a cheap model works just as well.

Fire Extinguishers. Since flare-ups are always a possibility when dealing with hot cooking fat, only a fool fails to have a tested fire extinguisher handy at all times while frying foods.

Ingredients

As this book clearly illustrates, there are not many foods that Southerners can't and don't fry, and since frying plays such an important role in our style of cooking, it stands to reason that as much attention is paid to the variety, distinct differences, and quality of ingredients as to the numerous principles and techniques involved in the frying process itself. Here is a rundown of the most essential ingredients and what to look for when planning to make most of the recipes.

Flour. Soft, winter, low-gluten Southern flour is different in texture from the high-protein hard-wheat variety that dominates in other parts of the country, and while many Southern cooks prefer to cook exclusively with Southern flour (especially for quick breads), regular unbleached all-purpose flour is perfectly acceptable for all the recipes in this book. (Soft-wheat flour can be ordered online from both White Lily Foods and King Arthur Flour Company.)

Cornmeal. Yellow or white cornmeal is an essential ingredient of numerous Southern fried dishes, batters, and coatings, and although the stone-ground varieties available in more and more fine markets have, without question, the best flavor and texture, regular commercial brands are suitable for all the recipes in this book that call for cornmeal. Some Southern cooks swear that white cornmeal is more refined than and superior to the yellow, but I say it's all simply a matter of personal taste.

Grits. There are two basic types of grits in the South: hominy grits, which are dried corn kernels with skins removed that are ground into a coarse meal, and plain, ordinary grits, which are the coarse grist of dried kernels with their skins. To complicate the semantics further, hominy (or "big hominy") by itself is soft, soaked whole grains of corn that are generally available in cans and marketed as a fine delicacy. The finest dried hominy grits are stone-ground and require at least 30 minutes' cooking time; and to really complicate matters, acceptable "quick grits" are regular grits that are processed to reduce cooking time to about 10 minutes, while dreadful "instant grits" are precooked, dehydrated, and flavored artificially to make them palatable. The recipes in this book deal primarily with hominy grits or plain whole hominy. When shopping, look for boxes or bags of regular grits or cans of hominy.

Rice and Potatoes. As essential to Southern cooking as cornmeal and grits since the days of the great Carolina and Georgia Lowcountry rice plantations, white and brown long-grain rice, which when cooked produces light, dry grains that separate easily, is now grown mainly in Louisiana, Arkansas, and Texas and is the commercial variety called for throughout this book. Short-grain rice, which is moist and viscous when cooked, has too high a starch content for these recipes, and never should any form of minute rice be substituted for the regular style of long-grain.

Generally, the best potatoes for frying are russets and long white varieties because of their low moisture and high starch content, and all fresh white potatoes should be firm, well shaped, and free of cracks, blemishes, and sprouts. Genuine fresh Southern sweet potatoes (which are not the same tuber as Latin American yams, despite erroneous marketing practices) have dark orange skins and a vivid orange, sweet flesh and are widely available during the cooler months. Sweet potatoes do not store as well as white ones, should never be refrigerated, and are best if used within a week of purchase.

Pork. Pig is the king of meats in the South, and while various cuts of pork are discussed in appropriate recipe headnotes throughout this book, special attention should be placed on bacon, sausage, and ham, all of which play a major role in so many Southern fried dishes. The preferred styles of bacon are cured, hickory-smoked slab bacon cut into relatively thick slices, lean salt pork (or "streak-o'-lean"), and dense, fragrant, woodsy artisanal bacon turned out by small, independent producers and increasingly available in all markets. When a recipe calls for sausage, the reference is to bulk pork sausage, and if you have trouble finding good commercial rolls in grocery stores outside the South, I've provided a recipe for making your own. Cured, well-aged country ham is available online for those who don't have local access to the specialized product, and even when country ham is indicated in a recipe, you can often use regular baked cured ham—with, of course, a sacrifice in flavor.

Poultry and Game. Frozen quail, rabbits, pheasant, and turkey parts are not only acceptable but also often preferable to the fresh products, but there's little excuse these days for using any chickens except the fresh commercial or organic ones available in all markets. Furthermore, serious Southern cooks frown on buying packaged chicken parts instead of whole chickens (with their giblets and livers), convinced justifiably that cutting up your own chickens (especially for fried chicken) guarantees both moister birds and better control over portions. All frozen game is quite perishable after being thawed, so keep refrigerated and use as soon as possible.

Seafood. With the exception of canned tuna and possibly salmon, as well as frozen crawfish tails and frogs' legs, only fresh seafood should be used for the recipes in this book. Unless otherwise indicated, shrimp and oysters should be medium-size, clams should be littlenecks or cherrystones, and crabmeat should be lump backfin. If frozen crawfish tails are unavailable for recipes that call for them, small shrimp can usually be substituted.

Vegetables. In the South, virtually any vegetable can be fried, and most Southern cooks are adamant about using only the freshest broccoli, cauliflower, eggplant, cabbage, squash, tomatoes, beans, mushrooms, parsnips, and greens. Exceptions might be sliced frozen okra and frozen corn kernels and black-eyed peas when the fresh don't look too good. Do note that all vegetables intended for frying should be patted dry, if necessary, even when dredged in flour or battered.

Nuts. Although chopped walnuts and toasted almonds are used occasionally in Southern fried dishes, by far the two most popular nuts called for in these recipes are peanuts and pecans. Small Georgia runner peanuts (the ones most often marketed commercially) are acceptable, but savvy Southern cooks know that nothing equals the large, oval, rich-tasting goobers grown in eastern North Carolina and Virginia, which are available online from a number of sources. Pecans are indigenous to the South and a key ingredient in multiple fried dishes. Since, however, fresh pecans quickly turn rancid, I'm very wary of the packaged nuts—even vacuum-sealed—sold in most markets. I order a good supply online every fall, and I store them in the refrigerator or freezer (up to one year).

Cheeses. Generally, "cheese" means only one thing in Southern cooking and that's cheddar and Parmesan, both of which are as important in many fried dishes as in other types of dishes. If I lay hands on a great artisanal Vermont or Canadian cheddar, so much the better, but for most of these recipes, any aged, extra-sharp commercial cheddar (yellow or white) is completely suitable. As for Parmesan, I use only genuine Parmigiano-Reggiano and recommend that you do the same.

Buttermilk. Long an indispensable staple of the Southern kitchen, buttermilk is not only used to flavor and leaven certain fried dishes but is also a key ingredient to many batters. Today, most buttermilk is pasteurized skim milk treated with an enzyme culture to make it sour, and while this is a far cry from the subtle, tangy buttermilk of yesteryear produced from fresh whole milk by natural fermentation, it nonetheless still plays an important role in fried foods. One bit of advice: If you forget to get a quart of buttermilk or run out, all-natural low-fat yogurt can be used very successfully in its place.

Sorghum and Molasses. Since quite a number of both savory and sweet fried dishes (rice pancakes, skillet cornbread, Texas cinnamon cookies, Creole calas) are often served with one of these syrups, no well-stocked Southern pantry is without a jar or can of sorghum or molasses (which can be used interchangeably). Sorghum is produced from a sweet grass and is usually referred to in the South simply as "syrup." Molasses is produced from the juice of sugarcane in varying grades, and the one to look for is pure, unsulfured molasses.

Batters, Breadings, and Seasonings

Batters and breadings not only insulate most fried foods from overcooking but are also the agents that produce the crispy and crunchy textures we all love. Not all fried items must be battered or breaded, but it's true that most are definitely too moist to brown evenly on their own without burning and that most can only benefit from a dusting of flour, possibly a quick dip in an egg wash, a light dredging in cornmeal or bread crumbs, or a full-fledged pancake-like coating (which, by itself, can even be used to make fritters, doughnuts, beignets, and nuggets of delectable fried dough). Most all composed batters contain flour, egg, leavening, and a thin liquid, but, as the many throughout this book illustrate, they can also include cornmeal, buttermilk, cream, melted butter, cooking oil, soy sauce, honey, seltzer, and beer. Breadings, on the other hand, are generally composed of only seasoned dry ingredients (flour, cornmeal, bread or cracker crumbs, and the like) that might be slightly moistened and intended to absorb the surface moisture of foods and produce a crisp, golden exterior finish while allowing interiors to cook completely. The quantity of batter or breading used for various foods affects both the flavor and texture of the item, so experiment carefully.

Many fried foods in this book call for a specific batter, but here is a recipe for an all-purpose batter that can be used (and modified) for all sorts of fried meats, poultry, seafood, vegetables, and rice dishes.

> 1½ cups all-purpose flour
> 1 teaspoon baking powder
> Salt and freshly ground black pepper to taste
> 1¼ cups milk
> 1 large egg
> 2 tablespoons vegetable oil

In a bowl, combine the flour, baking powder, and salt and pepper and stir till well blended. In a small bowl, whisk together the milk, egg, and oil till well blended, add to the dry ingredients, and beat till the batter is smooth. Pat dry with paper towels the food to be fried and dip each piece lightly or generously in the batter.

MAKES ABOUT 2 CUPS

As for seasoning batters with ingredients besides salt and pepper, possibilities include cayenne pepper, Tabasco sauce, Worcestershire sauce, mustard, vinegar, grated onion or cheese, garlic powder, ground nuts, and various herbs and spices. Note also that any fizzy liquid (beer, seltzer, soda, or sparkling wine) can be added to lighten many batters.

Frying Fats

The array of oils and other fats used to fry foods in the South is staggering, and virtually all are included in this book at some point. There is no firm rule governing which of the many fats available are best for any given foods, and while I may prefer the flavor (or lack of) and overall texture of one fat for a certain food, another similar one can often be substituted.

What matters most with all frying fats is their smoke point, meaning the stage at which heated fat begins to smoke, break down, emit acrid odors, and impart unpleasant flavors to foods. Fats have different smoke points (ranging from 350°F to 450°F). The higher the smoke point, the better suited a fat is for frying—still another reason to use a deep-fat thermometer as often as possible. Experienced Southern cooks grow up learning this major principle of frying, just as they learn that reusing fats and exposing them to air reduces smoke points. Depending on the amount of moisture in and the nature of the batter or coating on foods being fried, most fats can be used a second and possibly third time—no more—for the same items if carefully strained of loose particles and kept refrigerated. Any fat that smokes should be discarded, and all used fat should be smelled for rancidity before being reused. You should never reuse the same fat for frying different foods; you're only courting disaster to fry something like oysters and most vegetables in fat that was used to fry chicken; and I would never fry even sturdy foods such as sausage balls, soft-shell crabs, and whole quail in fat that was used to fry onion rings, cabbage, or hush puppies.

Generally, the best fats with the highest smoke points are canola, peanut, corn, soybean, safflower, and grapeseed oils, as well as lard and vegetable shortenings. The most inexpensive and popular brands of cooking oils are either blends of vegetable oils or exclusively canola or soybean, and all are suitable for all-purpose frying. Although each has its own distinctive aroma and flavor, I use a good deal of peanut and corn oils for frying seafood and chicken dishes, and I'd use more neutral-flavored grapeseed oil for vegetables and desserts if it were not so pricey. Olive oil might be trendy today in other styles of cooking, but since it has a low smoke point and aggressive flavor, it is not appropriate for frying most foods. Lard is wonderful for frying, and the best is pure, white, smooth leaf lard (from the fat around a pig's kidneys), which is available in small buckets at finer markets or from some butchers. Firmer, nutty, processed lard with a longer shelf life is also suitable so long as it's not off-colored and grainy, and, like all lard, it should be kept refrigerated as a safeguard against rancidity. Both butter and bacon grease have acceptable smoke points and, of course, sublime flavors, and so long as they're used in moderation, they are ideal for certain shallow-fried foods. Southerners like different fats for different reasons, and the only way to determine which appeals to you most is, as always, to experiment.

Cooking Guidelines and Techniques

In the South, "frying" does not mean grilling, pan-broiling, sautéing, browning, or even stir-frying. Southern frying is simply the age-old technique whereby foods are or are not battered or breaded and either submerged in hot, liquid fat and deep-fried, or shallow-fried in less fat. The goal of each method is to produce food that is usually fully set or golden brown and crispy on the surface, moist on the inside, not at all greasy, and utterly delectable. In this book, "deep frying" signifies more than 1 inch of hot cooking fat, whereas "shallow frying" implies less than 1 inch of fat. Whichever method is used, the cooking techniques are basically the same, with certain guidelines that should always be respected:

- Whether using a deep fryer, Dutch oven, deep skillet, or large saucepan, always allow 2 to 3 inches between the surface of the fat and the top of the vessel to prevent spillovers, excessive spattering, and possible fires.

- For deep frying, a sufficient amount of fat (usually at least a quart) is needed so that food is never crowded and browns evenly. Remember also that adding food to any hot fat cools down the fat, which must always be returned to the proper temperature to prevent the food (especially battered items) from soaking up the fat and becoming soggy.

- All food that is not battered or breaded should be patted dry before frying. Moistly battered food in a basket, slotted spoon, or spider should be lowered slowly into the fat to prevent sudden temperature drops and spattering.

- When frying food in a basket, periodically shake the basket carefully to prevent pieces from sticking. When shallow frying, use a slotted spoon or spider to separate pieces.

- Generally, smaller foods should be fried quickly at high temperature (at least 365°F), whereas larger and frozen items can often be fried at lower temperature (325°F to

350°F) to ensure that interiors are fully cooked while exteriors are brown and crisp. The higher the temperature, however, the less fat is absorbed in any food.

- To clarify any cooking fat for reuse, heat it slowly, strain through cheesecloth or coffee filters, and refrigerate till ready to use. Discard any cooking fat when it turns dark.

- When using any fresh fat for frying, allow an extra minute of cooking time until the first few items have been fried and the temperature of the fat has stabilized.

- Since debris in cooking fat can be responsible for frequent and wasteful fat changes, always shake off excess batter and breading before frying foods.

- To help moist batter adhere better to foods, dredge the battered pieces briefly in flour or cornmeal. To help dry breadings adhere better, add just enough beaten egg or buttermilk to the breading to firm it up slightly. Remember also that all batters and breadings adhere best when chilled for about 30 minutes after being used on foods.

- Never forget that batters and breadings can absorb huge amounts of fat and become soggy if the fat is not hot enough.

Frying Safeguards

Although there are potential dangers in the frying of any foods, nobody who takes obvious precautions, remains alert to possible mishaps, and uses plenty of common sense should encounter serious problems. Today, most deep fryers have every safety feature imaginable; heavy, sturdy cast-iron and stainless steel cookware minimizes the likelihood of stovetop accidents; and, as every Southern child learns while observing experienced adults fry up a skillet of chicken or pot of hush puppies, such habits as keeping vessels on the back of the stove with handles turned away and watching for smoke warnings from overheated fat are major safeguards against nasty burns and sudden fiery flare-ups.

What promotes hazards most are carelessly overfilling a vessel so that hot fat bubbles over the sides and comes in contact with the flame or element on your stove; allowing the fat to overheat, smoke, and possibly ignite; and dropping any significant amount of water or moist food into a container of hot fat, which could result in splattering, scalding, or even fire. In the case of smoking fat and excessive sputtering, reduce the heat immediately and allow the fat to cool. In case of serious fire, always have a tested fire extinguisher close by. And in case of a small, contained fire, never use water or flour to extinguish it but, rather, large amounts of baking soda—or even table salt. Most of all, never leave frying foods unattended, always watch carefully for any signs of danger or mishap, and maintain your composure as much with frying as with any other style of cooking.

The Health Issue

Depending strictly on how it is handled and the amounts consumed, fried food is no more or no less healthy than any other type of cooked food, and most fears today over eating a crunchy piece of fried chicken, a lightly fried crab cake, several corn fritters or hush puppies, or a luscious fried fruit turnover are either unwarranted, highly exaggerated, or utterly absurd. I could discourse boringly, for instance, on the components of various cooking fats (saturated and polyunsaturated oils, monounsaturated lard molecules, hydrogenated shortenings, trans fats, and so forth) and on how each might or might not affect our health and well-being. But, like most Southerners who for centuries have relished a diet chock-full of wonderful fried foods and somehow managed to survive the putative ravages of country ham with red-eye gravy, crispy oysters and okra, crusty pigs' ears and golden quail, and toothy rice croquettes, I frankly lose patience with overzealous fanatics who would have me and the rest of humanity nourish ourselves on nothing but grilled tofu, steamed sea bass, and sushi.

The truth is that, much as Southerners love fried foods and despite outside perceptions, we hardly eat them round the clock and frown as much as anybody else on the atrocious, commercial junk we encounter far too often outside the home. Savvy Southern cooks are also aware that, when cooked properly, deep- and shallow-fried foods absorb no more fat than those that are sautéed or stir-fried; that foods fried at a minimum temperature of 365°F absorb virtually no fat (hardly a tablespoon even with a big batch); that nothing absorbs more fat than over-battered foods fried at too low temperatures; and that, as always, moderation is the key to consuming delectable fried foods without inordinate concern over fats, cholesterol, sodium, calories, and all the other dietary evils that can make life so miserable. Prepared correctly, fried dishes are not heavy, greasy, soggy, or, indeed, unhealthy, and if this book imparts a simple undeniable fact, it is that lousy fried food can most often be attributed not to a series of dubious ingredients or age-old cooking techniques but to the person working the basket or wielding the slotted spoon.

Appetizers

Spicy Blistered Virginia Goobers

MAKES 4 CUPS

In a nutshell, no peanut anywhere equals the large, oval, rich-tasting goobers grown in Virginia and eastern North Carolina, and if you think ordinary roasted nuts are delicious, wait till you sample the mellow, intensely nutty, blistered variety found at many Southern cocktail receptions. Most likely, you'll have to order these raw nuts online from any number of sources, but if you're as obsessed with great peanuts as I am, it's well worth the effort and expense. Otherwise, any style of raw Spanish peanuts can be fixed in the same manner, so long as you watch them very carefully to make sure they don't darken too much and burn.

Peanut oil for deep frying
Tabasco sauce to taste

4 cups shelled raw peanuts (preferably
   Virginia or Carolina)
Salt to taste

In a large skillet, heat about 1 inch of oil seasoned with Tabasco to 350°F on a deep-fat thermometer, add 2 cups of the peanuts, fry just till the nuts are slightly darker, about 5 minutes, and drain on paper towels. Repeat with the remaining 2 cups of nuts and sprinkle with salt while still hot, turning the nuts. Let cool completely and either serve with cocktails or store in an airtight jar.

 The ideal vessel for frying should be large enough to allow 2 to 3 inches between the surface of the fat and the top of the vessel.

Tidewater Fried Oysters on Toasted Biscuits

MAKES 6 SERVINGS

Oysters battered in cornmeal and quickly fried are a staple all along the eastern seaboard from Maryland to Florida, but around Norfolk, Newport News, and Virginia Beach in Virginia's Tidewater area, one specialty is this dish: unbattered fried oysters that are spooned on biscuits with a delectable sherry cream sauce and served as a sit-down appetizer or elegant luncheon dish. What makes this such an easy dish is that the sauce can be prepared in advance and kept warm, meaning all you have to do is fry the oysters while the biscuits are toasting. This is one dish that should definitely be served hot, and I always make sure my sauce is well heated. By no means overcook these oysters, and you may not even have to turn them in the fat.

¼ pound bacon, finely chopped
1 scallion (white part only), minced
3 tablespoons dry sherry
2 tablespoons all-purpose flour
¾ cup heavy cream

2 teaspoons minced fresh tarragon
Salt and freshly ground black pepper to taste
Peanut oil for deep frying
2 dozen fresh oysters, shucked and drained
6 biscuits, broken in half and toasted

In a medium skillet, fry the bacon over moderate heat till almost crisp, add the scallion, and stir till the scallion is golden, about 2 minutes. Add the sherry, stir, and cook till reduced by half, about 2 minutes. Add the flour and whisk till well blended, about 1 minute. Stir in the cream, tarragon, and salt and pepper, simmer till the sauce is thickened, 3 to 4 minutes, and keep warm.

In a deep fryer or large, deep skillet, heat about 2 inches of oil to 375°F on a deep-fat thermometer, drop the oysters, a few at a time, into the oil, fry no more than 2 minutes or till golden brown, turning once, and drain on paper towels.

To serve, place 2 biscuit halves on each plate, top each serving with 4 oysters, and spoon the hot sauce over the tops.

Crunchy Cocktail Shrimp

MAKES 6 TO 8 SERVINGS

In the South, any occasion is right for fried shrimp, this zesty version being only one example of shrimp as the perfect cocktail food. The best way to crush the crackers is to place them in a plastic bag and roll with a rolling pin to a fairly fine consistency, and for a little extra flavor, you might want to substitute a more buttery cracker than saltines. This is one shrimp appetizer that calls for no sauce and is served simply with toothpicks. The recipe is equally delicious for small, shelled, thawed frozen crawfish if you're able to find some in the market.

½ cup buttermilk
1 large egg
½ teaspoon fresh lemon juice
¼ teaspoon Worcestershire sauce
Pinch of powdered dried fennel
1½ cups crushed saltine crackers

½ cup all-purpose flour
½ teaspoon salt
⅛ teaspoon cayenne pepper
Peanut or safflower oil for deep frying
2 pounds fresh shrimp, shelled and deveined

In a bowl, combine the buttermilk, egg, lemon juice, Worcestershire, and fennel, whisk together till well blended, and set aside.

In a shallow dish, combine the cracker crumbs, flour, salt, and cayenne, and mix till well blended.

In a large stainless steel or aluminum saucepan, heat about 2 inches of oil to 365°F on a deep-fat thermometer. Dip the shrimp in the buttermilk batter, dredge lightly in the crumb mixture, fry in batches in the oil till golden, about 2 minutes, and drain on paper towels.

Serve as hot as possible with toothpicks.

Sassy Shrimp Puffs

MAKES ABOUT 50 PUFFS

Southerners love any ground seafood that's mixed with moist bread and/or mashed potatoes, enhanced with various seasonings, and turned into balls, puffs, or nuggets for cocktail parties and stylish receptions. These tasty puffs could just as easily be made with ground clams, lobster, crawfish, crabmeat, or even a lean fish, but whatever seafood you use, just be careful not to over-fry the puffs. Don't ask me why, but for these types of puffs, I always use an electric frypan—as my mother always did.

5 slices white loaf bread, crusts removed
Milk
1 pound fresh shrimp, shelled, deveined, and finely ground

2 medium potatoes (about ½ pound), boiled and mashed
½ teaspoon powdered dried fennel
Salt and freshly ground black pepper to taste
Peanut oil for deep frying

Tear the bread into a bowl, add enough milk to moisten well, let soak for 10 minutes, squeeze dry, and place in a bowl, discarding the milk. Add the shrimp, mashed potatoes, fennel, and salt and pepper, mix with your hands till well blended and smooth, and form the mixture into 1-inch balls.

In a deep fryer or electric frypan, heat about 2 inches of oil to 365°F on a deep-fat thermometer, drop the balls into the oil in batches, fry till golden brown, about 2 minutes, and drain on paper towels.

Serve the puffs hot with plenty of toothpicks.

Deviled Cocktail Crab Cakes with Caper Tartar Sauce

MAKES 8 SERVINGS

In the South, anything "deviled" in cooking implies spicy ingredients such as dry (or hot) mustard, cayenne pepper, Tabasco sauce, and the like, and never is the concept more rewarding than when applied to ordinary crab cakes. Deviled crab cakes are a specialty in Maryland, and, if you prefer, you can use this mixture to make four main-course patties that can be served with no more than a sprinkling of fresh lemon juice, coleslaw, and some type of biscuit. On the other hand, I've noticed that nothing is a bigger hit on cocktail buffets than these small fried cakes dabbed with a little tartar sauce spiked with capers.

THE TARTAR SAUCE
1 cup mayonnaise
1 tablespoon grated onion
2 tablespoons drained capers, coarsely
  chopped
2 tablespoons finely chopped fresh parsley
  leaves
1 tablespoon coarsely chopped sweet pickles
Salt and freshly ground black pepper to taste

THE CRAB CAKES
½ cup half-and-half
½ cup mayonnaise
1 large egg white

1½ teaspoons dry mustard
2 teaspoons Worcestershire sauce
2 teaspoons fresh lemon juice
Tabasco sauce to taste
2 scallions (part of green tops included),
  minced
1 small red bell pepper, seeded and minced
½ teaspoon salt
1 pound fresh lump crabmeat, picked over for
  shell and cartilage
1 cup fine dry bread crumbs
1 tablespoon butter, melted
¼ cup peanut oil
2 tablespoons butter

To make the sauce, combine all the ingredients in a bowl and mix till well blended. Cover and refrigerate till ready to serve.

To make the crab cakes, whisk together the half-and half, mayonnaise, and egg white in a bowl till well blended. Add the dry mustard, Worcestershire, lemon juice, Tabasco, scallions, bell pepper, and salt and stir till well blended. Gently fold in the crabmeat and ½ cup of the bread crumbs till well blended.

Divide the mixture into 8 equal parts and shape each into a small cake. In a small bowl, combine the remaining ½ cup bread crumbs with the melted butter, mix well, and turn each cake in the mixture to coat lightly.

In a large, deep skillet, heat the oil and 2 tablespoons butter over moderate heat to 350°F on a deep-fat thermometer, add the crab cakes, and cook till lightly browned, about 3 minutes per side. Drain briefly on paper towels and serve with the tartar sauce.

 Crowding too much food in a vessel of hot oil causes the temperature of the oil to drop and the food to absorb maximum fat.

Crab and Corn Fritters Remoulade

MAKES ABOUT 1 DOZEN SMALL FRITTERS

W hile the mixture for these fritters can be formed into large oval patties, pan-fried in butter, and served as a main course with no more than lemon juice, what I really love to do is fry small fritters and serve them with a glorious remoulade dressing as an appetizer or buffet dish. Do notice that these fritters are shallow-fried in very little oil and should be cooked only till they're golden. Store leftover remoulade dressing in the refrigerator for future use with fried or boiled shrimp, cold vegetable salads, sliced tomatoes, and the like.

THE REMOULADE DRESSING
2 large egg yolks
¼ cup vegetable oil
½ cup finely chopped scallions
½ cup finely chopped celery
¼ cup chopped fresh parsley leaves
¼ cup prepared horseradish
¼ lemon, seeded and cut up (rind included)
1 bay leaf, crumbled
2 tablespoons Creole mustard
2 tablespoons ketchup
2 tablespoons Worcestershire sauce
1 tablespoon Dijon mustard
1 tablespoon white wine vinegar
1 tablespoon Tabasco sauce
1 tablespoon minced garlic
3 tablespoons drained capers
2 teaspoons sweet paprika
1 teaspoon salt

THE FRITTERS
1 cup yellow cornmeal
½ cup all-purpose flour
1½ teaspoons baking powder
1 teaspoon baking soda
Salt to taste
2 large eggs, beaten
½ cup buttermilk, plus more as needed
1½ tablespoons fresh lime juice
4 tablespoons (½ stick) butter
1½ cups corn kernels (fresh or thawed frozen)
½ cup finely chopped red bell pepper
2 scallions (part of green tops included), finely chopped
1 pound fresh lump crabmeat, picked over for shell and cartilage and flaked
Vegetable oil for shallow frying

(continued overleaf)

To make the dressing, place the yolks in a blender or food processor and blend for 1 minute. With the machine running, add the oil gradually in a thin stream till the emulsion is thickened. One at a time, add the remaining ingredients and process till well blended and the lemon rind is finely chopped. Transfer the dressing to a covered container and chill for at least 2 hours.

To make the fritters, combine the cornmeal, flour, baking powder, baking soda, and salt in a large bowl and stir till well blended. In a small bowl, combine the eggs, buttermilk, and lime juice and whisk till well blended. Add to the dry ingredients and stir till the batter is well blended and smooth.

In a medium skillet, melt the butter over moderate heat, add the corn, bell peppers, and scallions and cook, stirring, till softened, 4 to 5 minutes. Add the cooked vegetables and crabmeat to the batter, stir gently with a fork till well mixed, and form the mixture into small appetizer patties, adding a little more buttermilk if necessary for a smooth consistency.

In a large, heavy skillet, heat about ¼ inch of oil over moderately high heat, cook the patties till golden, 2 to 3 minutes on each side, and drain on paper towels.

Serve the fritters hot with the remoulade dressing.

✳ To prevent serious flare-ups, never drop any water or frozen foods with icicles into hot cooking fat.

Lowcountry Flounder Strips with Tartar Sauce

MAKES 4 TO 6 SERVINGS

No fish (except maybe catfish) is more loved in the South than flounder, and when it comes to the fine art of frying fish, no species is put more to the test than the sweet flounder served at the coastal seafood houses that dot the Carolina and Georgia Lowcountry. Of course the most popular dish is whole fried fillets served simply with butter and lemon juice as a main course, but equally relished are curly strips or fingers that are fried till crisp but still moist inside and served with a tangy tartar sauce at both casual and formal receptions. Any mild, lean white fish can be used to make these strips, and for more engaging flavor, use lard instead of shortening. To ensure that the exteriors don't brown too much before the interiors are cooked, do note that the fat should not register over 350°F.

THE TARTAR SAUCE
1 cup mayonnaise
2 teaspoons fresh lemon juice
1 scallion (white part only), minced
2 tablespoons coarsely chopped sweet pickles
2 tablespoons finely chopped fresh parsley
  leaves
Cayenne pepper to taste

THE FLOUNDER STRIPS
1 cup all-purpose flour
Salt and cayenne pepper to taste
2 large eggs
½ cup milk
2 pounds fresh flounder fillets
2 cups fresh bread crumbs
Vegetable shortening for deep frying
Freshly ground black pepper to taste

To make the tartar sauce, combine all the ingredients in a bowl, stir till well blended, cover with plastic wrap, and chill till ready to use.

To make the flounder strips, combine the flour and salt and cayenne on a plate and stir till well blended. In a bowl, whisk the eggs and milk together till well blended.

Cut the fish fillets into diagonal strips about ½ inch wide, dust them in the flour, dip into the egg mixture, then dredge lightly in the bread crumbs, pressing the crumbs into the fish.

In a deep fryer, electric frypan, or large, deep skillet, melt enough shortening to measure about 2 inches and heat to 350°F on a deep-fat thermometer. Drop the strips, a few at a time, into the fat, fry till golden brown, about 3 minutes, drain on paper towels, and season with salt and black pepper.

Serve hot with the tartar sauce on the side.

Bo's Dilled Conch Fritters

MAKES ABOUT 14 FRITTERS

Anyone who's walked down Duval Street in Key West, Florida, couldn't help but be aware of the stands offering fried, aromatic conch fritters, and when the small, tough mollusk indigenous to the Keys is properly tenderized, battered, and not overcooked, it's one of the South's most distinctive delicacies. The fritters can be seasoned with any number of ingredients, but perhaps the best I ever tasted were enhanced by a little fresh dill at a place called Bo's Fish Wagon. Fresh conch, which is highly perishable, is unlikely to be found outside the region, but the canned or frozen product available in more and more markets is completely acceptable and can easily be tenderized in a food processor. The slightly chewy fritters make not only an unusual appetizer but also a delectable luncheon dish when served with coleslaw, perhaps some pickled peaches, and hot corn sticks.

½ pound canned or frozen conch meat (if fresh, foot and orange fin removed)

2 tablespoons fresh lime juice

1 small onion, minced

½ small green bell pepper, seeded and minced

1 garlic clove, minced

1 tablespoon minced fresh dill

Salt and freshly ground black pepper to taste

Cayenne pepper to taste

1 large egg, beaten

1 cup whole milk

1 cup all-purpose flour

1 teaspoon baking powder

Vegetable oil for deep frying

Lime wedges for garnish

Dice the conch finely, place in a food processor, and grind till finely minced. Transfer to a glass bowl, add the lime juice, and toss well. Cover with plastic wrap and refrigerate for 30 minutes.

Add the onion, bell pepper, garlic, dill, salt and pepper, cayenne, egg, and milk to the minced conch and stir till well blended.

In a large bowl, combine the flour and baking powder and stir till well blended. Gradually add to the conch mixture, stir till a thick batter forms, cover, and refrigerate for 1 hour.

Preheat the oven to 250°F.

To fry the fritters, heat about 2 inches of oil in a heavy saucepan to 350°F on a deep-fat thermometer and, in batches, drop tablespoons of the conch batter into the oil. Turning frequently, fry till golden brown, 4 to 5 minutes, drain on paper towels, and keep warm in the oven till all the fritters are fried. Serve immediately with lime wedges to be squeezed over the tops.

Spicy Chicken Fingers

MAKES 6 SERVINGS

These fingers are spicy, but if you like even more intense flavor (as I do), you can coat them in the dry mixture, cover with plastic wrap, and refrigerate overnight. While I personally love the fingers just by themselves with no sauce, by all means feel free to serve them with a favorite sour-sweet sauce or dip or maybe a dilled mayonnaise. To ensure that the interiors cook through without the outsides burning, do not allow the oil to heat over 350°F, and be careful not to crowd the fryer or skillet with too many fingers at a time so that they'll cook evenly. As for serving the fingers, the hotter the better.

---

1 teaspoon dry mustard
1 teaspoon paprika
1 teaspoon garlic powder
Salt and freshly ground black pepper to taste
1½ pounds boneless, skinless chicken
    breasts, cut into 3 by 1-inch fingers

1 cup all-purpose flour
3 large eggs, beaten
2 cups cornmeal
Peanut oil for deep frying

In a bowl, combine the mustard, paprika, garlic powder, and salt and pepper and mix till well blended. Add the chicken fingers and toss till well coated.

Place the flour, eggs, and cornmeal in separate dishes.

In a deep fryer or large, deep skillet, heat about 2 inches of oil to 350°F on a deep-fat thermometer. In batches, dust the fingers in the flour, dip into the egg, dredge in the cornmeal, and fry till golden brown and crisp, about 3 minutes, turning once. Drain on paper towels and serve immediately.

Fried Chicken Drumettes Parmesan

MAKES 4 OR 5 SERVINGS

Most Southerners believe correctly that wings are the sweetest part of the chicken, and nothing is relished more on buffets and at cocktail parties than a platter of fried, spicy wings ("drumettes") enhanced with tangy Parmesan cheese and intended to be eaten with the fingers. If the wings are especially meaty, they may require a minute or so longer in the fat, but be careful not to fry them so much that the interiors dry out. Do feel free to experiment with various herbs and spices in this recipe. The wings are just as good at room temperature as they are hot.

---

12 to 15 chicken wings
1 cup all-purpose flour
½ cup grated Parmesan cheese
1 teaspoon paprika
½ teaspoon dry mustard

¼ teaspoon dried oregano, crumbled
Salt and freshly ground black pepper to taste
1 cup milk
Peanut oil for deep frying

To prepare the chicken wings, remove and discard the tips, separate the first and second joints with a sharp knife, and set the pieces aside.

In a shallow baking dish, combine the flour, cheese, paprika, mustard, oregano, and salt and pepper and stir till well blended.

Dip the chicken pieces in the milk, dredge in the flour mixture, tapping off excess flour, and place on a plate.

In a deep fryer, electric frypan, or Dutch oven, heat about 2 inches of oil to 365°F on a deep-fat thermometer. Fry the chicken pieces in batches for 8 minutes, turn with tongs, fry till golden brown, 6 to 8 minutes longer, and drain on paper towels.

Serve the drumettes hot or at room temperature.

 For the crispiest and least greasy fried chicken, drain the chicken pieces on wire racks or brown paper bags instead of paper towels.

Mississippi Fried Chicken Turnovers

MAKES 6 APPETIZER SERVINGS

Fried chicken turnovers are a popular appetizer (or main course) throughout the Deep South, but the best I ever tasted are these that my friend and neighbor Craig Claiborne's mother prepared when he was a child in Mississippi. The dough for the turnovers can be made with rendered chicken fat instead of butter, and the turnovers served with a creamed mushroom sauce in the old-fashioned tradition, but even I find these variations to be just too rich for modern appetites. If you prefer to serve the turnovers as a main course for four instead of an appetizer, cut the dough into 5- to 6-inch circles.

THE DOUGH
2 cups sifted cake flour
2 teaspoons baking powder
1 teaspoon salt
3 tablespoons butter (or chicken fat), softened
½ cup milk

THE TURNOVERS
2 tablespoons butter

2 tablespoons all-purpose flour
1½ cups half-and-half
2 large egg yolks, beaten
⅛ teaspoon grated nutmeg
½ teaspoon Worcestershire sauce
1½ cups coarsely chopped cooked chicken
Salt and freshly ground black pepper to taste
Corn oil for deep frying

To make the dough, combine the cake flour, baking powder, and salt in a bowl and stir till well blended. Add the butter and blend with a pastry blender till the mixture is mealy. Gradually add the milk, stir till the dough is soft and workable, cover with plastic wrap, and set aside.

To make the turnovers, melt the butter in a saucepan over moderate heat, add the flour, and whisk till well blended, about 1 minute. Whisking rapidly, add the half-and-half and whisk till well blended. Still whisking rapidly, pour a little of the hot sauce into the eggs, then return this mixture to the remaining sauce, whisking constantly. Add the nutmeg, Worcestershire, chicken, and salt and pepper, stir till well blended, and remove from the heat.

Turn the dough out onto a lightly floured surface and roll it out about ⅛ inch thick. Cut the dough into circles about 4 inches in diameter, spoon equal amounts of the filling into the centers, and fold the dough over to form crescents and enclose the filling. Press the edges securely to seal them.

In a deep fryer or large, deep skillet, heat about 2 inches of oil to 365°F on a deep-fat thermometer and fry the turnovers in batches till golden brown, 2 to 3 minutes on each side. Drain on paper towels and serve hot.

Fried Buttermilk–Chicken Livers

MAKES 4 TO 6 SERVINGS

F ried chicken livers (as well as gizzards) are relished in bars and even at fancy receptions all over the South, and ideally they should be slightly crunchy but still moist on the interior. As an appetizer, the livers are typically served with only a little Tabasco, but if you want something a bit more substantial, do as "Mama Dip" Council does at her namesake restaurant in Chapel Hill, North Carolina: Leave about a tablespoon of fat in the skillet after frying the livers, stir in 1 tablespoon of all-purpose flour plus $\frac{1}{2}$ cup of water, and serve the livers with the pan gravy. You could also make a sandwich with these.

---

1 pound chicken livers, trimmed of fat
1 cup buttermilk
2 cups all-purpose flour
$\frac{1}{2}$ teaspoon baking soda

Pinch of grated nutmeg
Salt and freshly ground black pepper to taste
Peanut oil for deep frying

In a bowl, combine the livers and buttermilk and let soak about for 5 minutes.

In a small baking dish, combine the flour, baking soda, nutmeg, and salt and pepper and mix till well blended.

In a deep cast-iron skillet, heat about 1½ inches of oil to 350°F on a deep-fat thermometer. Drain the livers, dredge each in the flour mixture, drop into the oil in batches, fry till golden brown and crunchy, about 3 minutes, turning once, and drain on paper towels.

Serve the livers hot or at room temperature.

Fried Pork Delights

MAKES ABOUT 20 COCKTAIL SERVINGS

All Southerners (and many Southern restaurants) have in their culinary repertory what are quaintly called "Oriental" dishes, and I don't know how long I've been playing around with these tangy pork nuggets that are marinated before being fried to a golden, slightly crispy finish. Served with any style of homemade or commercial barbecue sauce, the delights would certainly make a nice main course for four with lots of rice, but I personally think they're the perfect cocktail appetizer when eaten with toothpicks and dipped into a favorite barbecue sauce—or just Dijon mustard. Fry the delights just till they're golden; any longer and you risk their being tough.

---

1 cup soy sauce
1 cup dry sherry
1 garlic clove, minced
½ teaspoon freshly ground black pepper
¼ teaspoon dry mustard

One 1½-pound pork tenderloin, trimmed of fat and cut into 1-inch cubes
1 cup all-purpose flour
Salt to taste
Peanut oil for deep frying

In a large bowl, combine the soy sauce, sherry, garlic, pepper, and mustard and whisk till well blended. Add the pork, stir well, cover with plastic wrap, and refrigerate for at least several hours and preferably overnight.

In another small bowl, whisk together the flour and salt. Dredge the pork nuggets in the flour, shaking off the excess, and place on a large plate.

In a deep fryer or large, deep cast-iron skillet, heat about 2 inches of oil to 350°F on a deep-fat thermometer, fry the nuggets in batches till golden and slightly crisp, about 10 minutes, turning once, and drain on paper towels.

Serve hot on toothpicks with a favorite barbecue dipping sauce.

Company Sausage Balls

MAKES ABOUT 40 BALLS

Served traditionally in a chafing dish, sausage balls have been a staple at Southern cocktail receptions and on buffets for at least a century, and when they're not overly breaded or greasy, they make a delectable appetizer. The balls can be seasoned with anything from curry and chili powder to minced garlic to grated ginger and simply fried, or, as in this recipe, they can be enhanced even further by a zesty tomato sauce. To avoid greasiness, do note that the balls should always be fried in a well-drained skillet and never in a deep fryer, and be sure to serve them as hot as possible—preferably in a heated chafing dish. Stored in plastic bags, the uncooked balls freeze beautifully, making them the perfect last-minute solution to unexpected cocktail guests.

---

1 pound hot bulk pork sausage meat
1 large egg, beaten
½ cup fresh bread crumbs
2 teaspoons curry powder
½ teaspoon chili powder

Salt and freshly ground black pepper to taste
One 8-ounce can tomato sauce
¼ cup ketchup
1 tablespoon soy sauce
1 tablespoon Worcestershire sauce

In a bowl, break up the sausage with your hands, add the egg, bread crumbs, curry powder, chili powder, and salt and pepper, and mix till thoroughly blended. Form the mixture into 1–inch balls and place on a large plate.

In a large, deep skillet, fry the balls over moderate heat till nicely browned on all sides, 10 to 12 minutes, draining off fat as it accumulates. Drain the balls on paper towels.

In a large saucepan, combine the remaining ingredients and stir over moderate heat till well blended, about 2 minutes. Add the sausage balls, reduce the heat to low, cover, and simmer for about 15 minutes.

To serve, transfer the balls and sauce to a chafing dish to keep hot and provide plenty of toothpicks.

Beer-Battered Fried Onion Rings

MAKES 6 TO 8 SERVINGS

I n the South, there's virtually no occasion where fried onion rings are not appropriate—barbecues, burger cookouts, buffets, even formal dinners—and Southerners learned long ago that nothing's better to nibble on with strong cocktails than a basket of salty-sweet, crisp fried onions. Unlike those made with a milk batter, these rings dipped in a batter containing beer laced with baking powder are feather-light and almost zesty; and for the best flavor, lard is the preferred frying fat. Never allow the temperature of the fat to fall below 375°F if you want really crisp rings, and be sure to skim bits of batter from the fat between batches before they burn.

1½ cups all-purpose flour
½ teaspoon baking powder
½ teaspoon salt, plus more for sprinkling
One 12-ounce bottle of beer

2 large Spanish onions, peeled and sliced into
  ¼-inch-thick rings
Lard or vegetable oil for deep frying

In a bowl, combine the flour, baking powder, ½ teaspoon of salt, and beer. Stir till well blended, cover, and let the batter stand for about 1 hour.

Preheat the oven to 250°F. Line a large baking sheet with paper towels and set aside.

Dip the onion rings into the beer batter and place on a large plate. In a deep fryer or Dutch oven, heat about 2 inches of lard or oil to 375°F on a deep-fat thermometer. Drop 4 or 5 onion rings into the fat, fry till golden brown, about 1 minute, drain on paper towels, and keep warm in the oven while frying the remaining onion rings. Sprinkle with salt and serve hot.

Fried Okra with Thousand Island Dressing

MAKES 6 TO 8 SERVINGS

Originally, I used this recipe to make okra fritters to be served as part of a meal, but then I got the idea of frying the sliced pods as an appetizer for cocktail parties and small receptions. Suffice it to say that I defy even the most squeamish non-Southerners to eat these crunchy rounds and not proclaim that they love okra. As I always warn, this dish cannot be made successfully with frozen okra, so if you can't find firm, fresh pods in the market, opt for another appetizer.

THE DIP
1 cup mayonnaise
¼ cup bottled chili sauce
¼ cup minced pimento-stuffed green olives
1 large hard-boiled egg, finely chopped
1 tablespoon minced fresh chives
1 tablespoon minced green bell pepper
Tabasco sauce to taste

THE OKRA
1½ pounds firm, fresh okra, rinsed

¾ cup minced onion
¼ cup minced green bell pepper
3 tablespoons all-purpose flour
½ teaspoon salt
Freshly ground black pepper to taste
2 cups yellow cornmeal
1 large egg
2 tablespoons half-and-half
Tabasco sauce to taste
Lard or vegetable shortening for deep frying

To make the dip, combine all the ingredients in a small bowl, mix till well blended, cover, and chill till ready to use.

To make the okra, stem and slice it into ½-inch rounds. In a large bowl, combine the okra, onion, bell pepper, flour, salt, and pepper and toss till well blended. Add the cornmeal and toss again. In a small bowl, whisk together the egg, half-and-half, and Tabasco till well blended, pour over the okra rounds, stir gently, and let stand for about 15 minutes.

In a large skillet, melt about 1 inch of lard or shortening to 365°F on a deep-fat thermometer, drop the okra rounds in batches into the fat, and fry till golden brown, about 1 minute on each side. With a slotted spoon, transfer the rounds to paper towels to drain, then serve hot with toothpicks and the dip.

Carolina Sweet Potato Fritters

MAKES 6 TO 8 SERVINGS

While fried sweet potatoes are becoming trendy even in upscale restaurants all over the country, they've been a staple in North Carolina (and elsewhere in the South) at cocktail parties and with soups and salads for as long as anybody can remember. Fritters are the most popular form, but the potatoes can also be cut into oblongs, thin cylinders, or sticks like French fries—with the frying time adjusted according to thickness. Fried sweet potatoes tend to become limp and soggy much faster than regular potatoes, so be sure to serve them just as soon as possible after frying, and never cover the potatoes while keeping them warm in the oven.

---

4 medium sweet potatoes
1 cup all-purpose flour
1 teaspoon baking powder
¼ teaspoon grated nutmeg
Salt and freshly ground black pepper to taste

1 large egg, beaten
1 cup milk
2 tablespoons vegetable oil
Corn oil for deep frying

Place the potatoes in a large saucepan and add enough water to cover. Bring to a boil, reduce the heat slightly, and cook for 20 minutes. When cool enough to handle, peel the potatoes, slice ¼ inch thick, and pat dry with paper towels.

Preheat the oven to 250°F.

In a bowl, combine the flour, baking powder, nutmeg, and salt and pepper and stir till well blended. In a small bowl, whisk together the egg, milk, and vegetable oil till well blended, add to the dry mixture, and beat till the batter is smooth.

In a deep fryer or large, deep skillet or saucepan, heat about 1½ inches of corn oil to 375°F on a deep-fat thermometer. Dip the potato slices, a few at a time, into the batter, drop into the fat, fry till golden brown, about 2 minutes on each side, and drain on paper towels. Sprinkle salt on top, keep warm in the oven (do not cover) while other potatoes are frying, and serve immediately.

Hoppin' John's Fried Squash Blossoms

MAKES 6 TO 8 SERVINGS

One of Charleston, South Carolina's most respected chefs, "Hoppin' John" Taylor, knows a thing or two about frying foods, but never was I more impressed than when he came up with the idea of frying yellow squash blossoms as an unusual and delectable summer appetizer. Most likely, you'll find the attached blossoms only at farmers' markets, and if these are not available, look for zucchini, pumpkin, or melon blossoms. Since the blossoms are pretty bland, be sure to use lard (or possibly a classic olive oil) as a frying fat for optimum flavor. As for technique, the blossoms should be simply held by the stems and dipped into the hot fat just till they begin to brown.

1 large egg
1 cup ice water
1 cup unbleached all-purpose flour
Lard for deep frying

2 dozen yellow squash blossoms with stems attached
Salt to taste

Preheat the oven to 250°F.

In a wide bowl, combine the egg and ice water and beat with a wooden spoon till well blended. Add the flour all at once, stirring quickly till the batter is just lumpy.

In a Dutch oven or deep skillet, heat about 2 inches of lard to 365°F on a deep-fat thermometer.

Rinse and pat dry the squash blossoms; then, holding them by the stems, dredge in the batter. Plunge the blossoms in batches into the hot fat and fry for 30 seconds. Flip them over and fry till they begin to brown, about 15 seconds longer. Drain on a wire rack placed on top of a baking sheet and keep warm in the oven till all the blossoms are fried. Sprinkle the blossoms with salt and serve immediately.

Louisville Cheddar Fries

MAKES 12 TO 16 FRIES

Legend has it that these snappy cheddar fries originated as a bar snack in Louisville, Kentucky, to entice customers to drink more, and once you've tasted one, you'll understand why they can become so addictive. Traditionally, the small fries are rectangles or triangles, but I've also used the cheese mixture to make rounds, rolls, strips, or fingers, adjusting the frying time slightly according to thickness. This is also one time I prefer to fry in appropriately bland canola oil, since it has little effect on the luscious cheese flavor and is very low in saturated fat. Be sure to use aged, extra-sharp cheddar for these fries. I think the fries are good either warm or cooled.

4 tablespoons (½ stick) butter
¼ cup all-purpose flour
1 cup milk
½ pound extra-sharp cheddar cheese, ground or finely grated

Cayenne pepper to taste
½ cup cracker crumbs
2 large eggs, beaten
Canola oil for deep frying

In a large, heavy saucepan, melt the butter over moderate heat, add the flour, and whisk till well blended. Whisking, add the milk, bring to a boil, return the heat to moderate, and whisk till the sauce is thickened, about 5 minutes. Add the cheese and cayenne, stir till the cheese has melted, remove from the heat, and allow the mixture to cool till thickened.

Spread the mixture about 1 inch thick on a baking sheet, cover with plastic wrap, and chill for at least 2 hours in the refrigerator.

Cut the mixture into small rectangles or triangles, dredge the pieces lightly in the crumbs, dip them into the egg, and dredge again lightly in the crumbs.

In a deep fryer or large, deep skillet, heat about 2 inches of oil to 375°F on a deep-fat thermometer, drop the cheese pieces, a few at a time, in the oil, fry till golden brown, about 2 minutes, and drain on paper towels till cooled.

Eggs and Cheese

Perfect Fried Eggs

MAKES 1 SERVING

Fried eggs are so important in the South (with fried country ham and buttered grits at breakfast, on top of various hashes, and, indeed, as filling for a tasty sandwich), that it's often said that a cook who can't fry perfect eggs can't prepare anything. Here is the classic Southern way to fry eggs that have moist whites with yolks that are still soft. Another acceptable option is to add a teaspoon of water to the skillet, cover the eggs (preferably with aluminum foil), and steam-fry them for about 2 minutes or till the whites are just set and the yolks slightly opaque.

2 tablespoons butter or bacon grease
2 large eggs

Salt and freshly ground pepper to taste

In a large, heavy skillet, heat the butter or bacon grease over moderate heat for about 1 minute and crack the eggs into the skillet, spacing them so they don't run together. Reduce the heat to low, baste the eggs with the fat, and fry till the whites are set but the yolks still soft, about 2 minutes. Transfer to a serving plate and season with salt and pepper.

Fried Deviled Eggs

MAKES 6 SERVINGS

Only a Southern cook would come up with a technique for battering and frying the same deviled eggs that appear at every picnic and fried chicken dinner throughout the South, and if you think the idea is crazy, hold the criticism till you've tasted the crispy wonders that literally melt in the mouth and make such an unusual luncheon or brunch dish served with country ham biscuits and a congealed salad. Do try to serve these eggs as hot as possible, since they lose much of their savor when allowed to cool.

1 dozen large hard-boiled eggs
½ cup mayonnaise
1 tablespoon Dijon mustard
1 tablespoon chopped fresh chives
Salt and freshly ground black pepper to taste

Peanut oil for deep frying
1 cup all-purpose flour
1 large egg, beaten
1 cup fine bread crumbs

Cut the boiled eggs in half lengthwise and place the yolks in a bowl. Add the mayonnaise, mustard, chives, and salt and pepper and mash with a wooden spoon till well blended and smooth. Fill the egg whites with the yolk mixture and set aside.

In a deep fryer, heat about 2 inches of oil to 350°F on a deep-fat thermometer.

Dredge the stuffed eggs lightly in the flour, dip into the beaten egg, and dredge lightly in the bread crumbs. With a slotted spoon, lower the eggs in batches into the hot oil, fry till golden brown, turning once, 3 to 4 minutes, and drain on paper towels. Serve hot.

Cajun Crawfish Omelette

MAKES 4 SERVINGS

Every year at the crawfish festival held the first weekend of May in Breaux Bridge, Louisiana, local cooks compete to produce the most sumptuous crawfish dishes possible, and none ever impressed me more than this rich, smooth omelette with tangy cheddar melting all over the top. It's still not that easy to find fresh crawfish tails outside the region, but the frozen ones are fully acceptable, and, of course, small fresh shrimp can always be substituted. Be sure to fry this omelette only till the egg mixture is set but still moist.

2 tablespoons butter
1 small onion, finely chopped
1 celery rib, finely chopped
½ small green bell pepper, seeded and finely chopped
½ pound fresh or frozen crawfish tails

Salt and freshly ground black pepper to taste
Tabasco sauce to taste
5 large eggs
2 scallions (part of green tops included), chopped
½ cup grated extra-sharp cheddar cheese

In a medium skillet, melt the butter over moderate heat, add the onion, celery, and bell pepper, and stir till softened, about 5 minutes. Add the crawfish, salt and pepper, and Tabasco and continue stirring for 3 to 4 minutes. Remove from the heat.

In a bowl, beat the eggs till frothy, add the scallions plus salt and pepper, stir till well blended, and set aside.

Spread the crawfish mixture over the bottom of a large, heavy skillet and cook over moderate heat for 1 minute. Pour the egg mixture over the top, tip the pan to distribute the eggs evenly, and fry till the mixture is set, about 5 minutes, loosening the edges with a spatula.

To serve, transfer the omelette to a warm serving plate, cut it into wedges, and sprinkle the cheese over the tops.

Antoine's Spanish Omelette with Creole Sauce

MAKES 1 SERVING

Even my Swedish grandmother in North Carolina used to make what Southerners call a "Spanish omelette," but surely the most famous example is the one served for lunch at Antoine's restaurant in New Orleans, complete with a zesty Creole sauce spooned over the top. Ideally, each omelette should be soft-fried separately in the French manner, but, if you like, you can double the egg mixture and cut the omelette in half to make two servings. The omelette needs only a couple of tablespoons of sauce, and the remaining sauce should be reserved for other egg dishes or for steamed cauliflower, broccoli, and squash.

THE SAUCE
2 tablespoons butter
1 medium onion, finely chopped
1 small green bell pepper, seeded and finely chopped
2 medium ripe tomatoes, peeled and coarsely chopped
4 large garlic cloves, minced
¼ teaspoon dried thyme, crumbled
2 bay leaves
2 tablespoons minced fresh parsley leaves

1 teaspoon paprika
Salt and freshly ground black pepper
1 tablespoon cornstarch
3 tablespoons water

THE OMELETTE
4 tablespoons (½ stick) butter
⅓ cup sliced fresh mushrooms
3 large eggs
Salt and freshly ground black pepper to taste
⅓ cup cooked green peas

To make the sauce, melt the butter in a saucepan over moderate heat, add the onion and bell pepper, and stir till softened, 2 to 3 minutes. Add all remaining ingredients except the cornstarch and water, stir well, reduce the heat to low, and simmer for 20 minutes. In a small bowl, whisk the cornstarch in the water, blend it into the sauce, stir till thickened, and keep warm.

To make the omelette, melt 2 tablespoons of the butter in a small skillet, add the mushrooms, stir for 2 to 3 minutes, and set aside. In a bowl, whisk the eggs with salt and pepper, add the mushrooms and peas, and set aside.

In a large skillet, melt the remaining 2 tablespoons butter over moderately low heat, add the egg mixture, cook till set but still creamy, and carefully fold one half over the other half. Turn the omelette out onto a heated plate, spoon a few tablespoons of sauce over the top, and serve immediately.

Tar Heel Sweet Potato Omelette

MAKES 2 SERVINGS

Since North Carolina is the country's largest producer of sweet potatoes, there's little that Tar Heel cooks can't and don't do to highlight the noble spuds, like incorporating them in soft-fried omelettes such as this one intended for a casual Sunday supper and served with maybe leftover succotash and some toasted buttermilk biscuits. Notice that, as with most Southern omelettes, this one is not rounded and puffy in the French style, but fried till the edges brown slightly and then simply folded in half.

4 tablespoons (¹/₂ stick) butter
2 small sweet potatoes, peeled and diced
2 tablespoons minced fresh chives

4 large eggs
3 tablespoons milk
Salt and freshly ground black pepper to taste

In a large, heavy skillet, melt 2 tablespoons of the butter over low heat, add the sweet potatoes, and cook, stirring, till the potatoes are soft and lightly browned, about 20 minutes. Add the chives and stir well.

In a bowl, whisk the eggs and milk together till frothy, add the sweet potatoes plus salt and pepper, and stir till well blended.

In a large, heavy skillet, melt the remaining 2 tablespoons butter over moderate heat, add the egg mixture, and cook till the eggs begin to set and the omelette turns slightly brown at the edges. With a spatula, fold one half of the omelette over the other half, cut in half, and slide each half onto heated serving plates.

Tarragon Egg Croquettes

MAKES 6 SERVINGS

These zesty breakfast or brunch croquettes illustrate how creative deep frying can be when simple chopped hard-boiled eggs are combined with various seasonings, formed into small cylinders, and fried quickly to a golden, crispy finish. Do feel free to experiment with other herbs and even spices, and don't discount the idea of also serving the croquettes with maybe ham biscuits and an avocado salad for a casual supper. The croquettes should be served as hot as possible, though I do frown on covering them while they drain, since this can make them a little soggy.

4 tablespoons (½ stick) butter
1¼ cups all-purpose flour
1 cup milk
8 large hard-boiled eggs, finely chopped
2 scallions (part of green tops included), finely chopped
2 tablespoons finely chopped fresh parsley leaves

1 tablespoon finely chopped fresh tarragon leaves
1 teaspoon dry mustard
Salt and cayenne pepper to taste
1 cup fine fresh bread crumbs
1 large egg, beaten
Vegetable oil for deep frying

In a large, heavy skillet, melt the butter over moderate heat, add ¼ cup of the flour, and whisk till pasty. Whisking steadily, add the milk gradually and stir till the sauce thickens and is smooth. Remove the skillet from the heat, add the chopped eggs, scallions, parsley, tarragon, mustard, and salt and cayenne and stir till well blended. Scrape the mixture onto a large plate, cover with plastic wrap, and refrigerate for several hours to firm up.

Divide the mixture into cylinders about 3 inches long and 1 inch in diameter and place on a large plate. Spread the remaining 1 cup flour on another plate and the bread crumbs on another. Lightly dredge the croquettes in the flour, dip them into the beaten egg, then roll them in the bread crumbs. Cover with plastic wrap and refrigerate for about 30 minutes to firm up further.

In a deep fryer or large cast-iron skillet, pour about 2 inches of oil and heat to 350°F on a deep-fat thermometer. Add the croquettes 4 at a time and fry till golden brown and crisp on all sides, about 4 minutes, turning them once with a slotted spoon. Drain on paper towels and serve hot.

Kentucky Scramble

MAKES 4 SERVINGS

I n some Southern states, a "scramble" can imply a baked layered breakfast casse-role including hard-boiled eggs, sausage, and other ingredients, but in Kentucky, the term generally refers simply to soft-scrambled eggs with corn kernels and chopped onion, bell pepper, and pimentos served with fried bacon strips over the top. It's a sumptuous variation of scrambled eggs and the perfect dish for an unusual break-fast buffet or brunch. By no means overcook these eggs; they should be very soft and almost creamy. And do try to use fresh corn kernels scraped from the cobs (their milk included).

---

8 slices lean bacon
1 small onion, finely chopped
$\frac{1}{2}$ small green bell pepper, cored, seeded,
  and finely chopped

1 cup fresh or thawed frozen corn kernels
$\frac{1}{4}$ cup finely chopped pimentos
Salt and freshly ground black pepper to taste
6 large eggs

In a large, heavy skillet, fry the bacon over moderate heat till crisp, drain on paper towels, and reserve.

Pour off all but 3 tablespoons of fat from the skillet, add the onion, bell pepper, and corn, and stir till the vegetables are soft but not brown, about 5 minutes. Add the pimentos and salt and pepper and stir for 1 minute longer.

In a bowl, beat the eggs till frothy, pour them over the vegetables in the skillet, and stir over moderately low heat till the eggs begin to form soft, creamy curds.

To serve, mound the eggs on a heated platter, arrange the reserved bacon strips over the top, and serve immediately.

Georgia Bacon and Eggs with Hominy

MAKES 4 SERVINGS

Hominy is dried corn kernels that are soaked (usually in lye) to remove the tough skins, and while soft hominy is used throughout the South to make various side dishes and casseroles, never did I love it more than when relatives in Macon and Monticello, Georgia, served it simply with soft-scrambled eggs and thick fried crumbled bacon at the type of elaborate breakfast that all Southerners still relish. One aunt was so proud of her hominy and eggs that she always served them in a silver chafing dish. Today, I also serve this dish on brunch buffets, and there's never a morsel left. Just don't overcook the eggs.

4 thick slices bacon
One 16-ounce can hominy, drained

4 large eggs
Salt and freshly ground black pepper to taste

In a large skillet, fry the bacon over moderate heat till crisp, drain on paper towels, crumble, and reserve.

Pour off all but about 2 tablespoons of fat from the skillet, add the hominy, and stir till golden, about 5 minutes. In a bowl, whisk together the eggs and salt and pepper till frothy, add to the hominy, reduce the heat to low, and stir till the eggs are set but still moist, 5 to 7 minutes.

Transfer the eggs and hominy to a serving bowl, sprinkle the reserved bacon over the top, and serve immediately.

Sweet Ma's Brains and Eggs

MAKES 4 SERVINGS

For generations, brains and eggs have been considered a great delicacy in the South, and if outsiders cringe at the very idea, it's only because they've never tasted the rich, subtle dish still featured on more sophisticated brunch buffets. Even I objected to those strong hog brains my Georgia grandmother used to scramble with eggs for weekend breakfasts, but mild, delicate calf brains (available fresh or frozen in many Southern markets) are another matter altogether. Since you're not likely to find any brains outside the South, do note that frozen calf sweetbreads make a very acceptable substitute. Like brains, however, all sweetbreads are highly perishable once thawed and must be cooked within 24 hours.

---

1 pound calf brains or calf sweetbreads (fresh or thawed frozen)
1 tablespoon fresh lemon juice
1 tablespoon bacon grease
1 cup water

1 teaspoon salt
Freshly ground black pepper to taste
6 tablespoons (¾ stick) butter, cut into pieces
8 large eggs

To prepare the brains or sweetbreads, rinse them carefully under cold water, place in a bowl, add water to cover plus the lemon juice, and let soak for about 2 hours in the refrigerator. Drain, gently peel off and discard as much of the thin membrane as possible, and dry carefully with paper towels.

In a large skillet, heat the bacon grease over moderately low heat, add the prepared brains or sweetbreads, the water, salt, and pepper, and simmer, uncovered, till the water has evaporated, about 20 minutes. Remove from the heat.

When ready to serve, turn the heat to low, add the butter to the skillet, and, when it has melted around the brains or sweetbreads, add the eggs, stir gently, and scramble over low heat just till the eggs are set and slightly soft. Transfer to a warm bowl and serve immediately.

Classic Southern Cheese Omelette

MAKES 1 SERVING

Whether prepared for breakfast or a light Sunday supper, a traditional fried Southern cheese omelette (made with cheddar, Swiss, Parmesan, or even feta) is just the opposite of a rolled, puffy, slightly runny French omelette prepared quickly over high heat in a special omelette pan. Not that a Southern country-style omelette is necessarily dry and crisp around the edges from overcooking, but Southerners do like their omelettes relatively firm and folded in half, and what matters most is that the omelette be allowed to sit long enough in the skillet so that the cheese melts slowly and oozes out the sides. And if you want to taste something really unusual and sensual, make this omelette with pimento cheese added at room temperature to the beaten eggs. Now that's Southern!

---

1 tablespoon butter
3 large eggs
1 tablespoon heavy cream

Salt and freshly ground black pepper to taste
3 tablespoons grated extra-sharp cheddar
  cheese

In a medium, heavy skillet, melt the butter over moderate heat till bubbly but not brown. In a bowl, beat the eggs, cream, and salt and pepper with a fork till frothy, add the cheese, and stir till well blended. Pour into the skillet and draw the edges of the eggs toward the center. When the eggs are set, after about 1 minute, fold the omelette in half with a spatula, let stand in the pan for about 30 seconds longer, transfer to a serving plate, and serve immediately.

Paw Paw's Skillet Cheese and Eggs

MAKES 6 TO 8 SERVINGS

Give my Georgia grandfather a cast-iron skillet, and there was no limit to the fried dishes he would come up with. Paw Paw was one of those Southern cooks who elevated fried foods to unimaginable heights, and no dish exemplified his gift more than these luscious skillet eggs with cheese that I still prepare for special holiday breakfasts and serve ceremoniously in a silver chafing dish. The very finest extra-sharp cheddar cheese should be used for perfect results, and do note that if you rush the roux or cook the eggs too quickly over heat that's too high, you could end up with a lumpy disaster. The dish is easy to prepare, but it does require patience.

8 tablespoons (1 stick) butter
8 slices white loaf bread, trimmed and torn into pieces
1½ cups whole milk, plus more as needed
1½ pounds extra-sharp cheddar cheese, coarsely grated

10 large eggs, beaten
Salt and freshly ground black pepper to taste
Cayenne pepper to taste

In a large, heavy skillet, melt the butter over moderately low heat, then add the bread and milk and mash steadily and thoroughly with a sturdy fork till the mixture has the consistency of a soft roux, adding more milk if necessary. Add the cheese and continue mashing and stirring till the cheese is well incorporated and the mixture is very smooth. Add the eggs, salt and pepper, and cayenne pepper and stir slowly and steadily with a large spoon till the eggs are set and the mixture is almost creamy. (If the mixture seems to be sticking to the bottom of the skillet, lower the heat while stirring.)

Serve the cheese and eggs piping hot in a chafing dish or large heated bowl.

Appalachian Country Ham and Cheese Omelette

MAKES 2 SERVINGS

T he very finest dry-cured Southern country hams are produced in Virginia, West Virginia, North Carolina, Kentucky, and Tennessee, and I've been playing around with this robust omelette ever since I tasted one like it at a rustic café not far from the famous Greenbrier resort high in the Appalachians of West Virginia. Even in the South, it's no longer that easy to find truly superior country ham in regular markets, and much of the packaged commercial product is aged no more than a month or so. Expensive slices of Smithfield ham, available in finer markets around the country, are always a good possibility. Otherwise, try to find well-cured local ham that is not too thin and has fat that is more creamy than white in color—the same style of lusty ham that is fried for breakfast and served with red-eye gravy.

$^1/_4$ cup all-purpose flour
$^1/_4$ cup white cornmeal
2 pinches onion powder
2 pinches garlic powder
Salt and freshly ground black pepper to taste
1 medium green tomato, cored and thinly sliced

9 tablespoons butter
6 large eggs
$^1/_4$ pound lean country ham, chopped
1 cup grated Swiss cheese
1 teaspoon chopped fresh chives
$^1/_2$ teaspoon chopped fresh parsley leaves
$^1/_4$ teaspoon chopped fresh tarragon leaves

In a wide, shallow bowl, combine the flour, cornmeal, onion powder, garlic powder, and salt and pepper and stir till well blended. Dredge the tomato slices in the mixture. In a medium skillet, melt 3 tablespoons of the butter over moderate heat, add the coated tomato slices, and fry till golden, about 2 minutes on each side. Remove from the skillet and set aside.

Crack 3 of the eggs into a small bowl and beat well. Melt 3 more tablespoons of the butter in the skillet over moderate heat, add half the ham, and cook, stirring, for 1 minute. Pour the eggs over the ham and stir till wet curds form. Scatter half the cheese and half the fried tomatoes over the top, sprinkle half the chives, parsley, and tarragon over the top, and cook till the eggs are just set, about 1 minute. With a spatula, flip one half of the omelette over the other half, let sit for 1 minute, then transfer to a heated plate.

Repeat the process with the remaining ingredients to make a second omelette.

Fried Breakfast Cheese

MAKES 2 TO 4 SERVINGS

Charlotte, North Carolina, has always had a large Greek community and any number of family restaurants and diners run by Greeks, and one of the many dishes the chefs have transformed over the years to fit the Southern repertory is the fried cheese (*saganaki*) often served at breakfast. Any semihard cheese can be fried in this manner, but nothing is more Southern and luscious than a full-flavored, well-aged cheddar that has just the right melting consistency. These triangles are also a big hit on the buffet table.

$1/2$ cup all-purpose flour
2 teaspoons dried oregano, crumbled
Freshly ground black pepper to taste

$1/2$ pound extra-sharp cheddar cheese
$1/2$ cup olive oil
2 lemon halves, seeded

On a plate, combine the flour, oregano, and pepper and stir till well blended. Cut the cheese into eight 3 by 2-inch triangles about $1/2$ inch thick, dredge in the flour mixture, and set aside.

In a medium, heavy skillet, heat the olive oil to 365°F on a deep-fat thermometer and, working in batches, fry the cheese triangles till just melted and golden on both sides, 2 to 3 minutes, turning once. Transfer to a serving plate and squeeze lemon juice over the tops.

 To avoid spatters while frying, always lower foods gradually into the fat.

New Orleans Blue Cheese Beignets

MAKES 4 TO 6 SERVINGS

Inspired by the sweet yeast doughnuts served with strong chicory coffee in the French Market of New Orleans, these savory beignets illustrate how imaginative Creole chefs can transform one local fried specialty into another, altogether different concept that's so perfect for buffet receptions, bridge luncheons, or a first course at dinner. To prevent oozing, be sure to seal the edges of the beignets securely and chill them well before frying. You could also fill these beignets with curried minced cooked chicken or caramelized chopped onions.

THE PASTRY
- 1 envelope active dry yeast
- $1/4$ cup warm water
- 2 tablespoons sugar
- $2^1/2$ cups all-purpose flour
- 1 teaspoon salt
- 8 tablespoons (1 stick) butter, cut into pieces
- 2 large eggs plus 2 large egg yolks, at room temperature

THE BEIGNETS
- 1 pound blue cheese, at room temperature
- $1/4$ cup all-purpose flour
- 2 large eggs
- 3 tablespoons water
- $1/2$ teaspoon salt
- Pinch of grated nutmeg
- Vegetable oil for deep frying
- 2 tablespoons capers, rinsed and chopped

To make the pastry, combine the yeast and water in a small bowl and let proof for 10 minutes.

In a food processor, combine the sugar, flour, salt, and butter and process till the butter is incorporated into the flour, about 30 seconds. Add the yeast mixture, pulse 2 or 3 times, add the eggs and egg yolks, and process till the liquid is incorporated. Scrape the sides of the bowl and process for 1 minute longer to knead the dough. Scrape the dough into a greased bowl, shape into a ball, cover with a towel, and let rise in a warm area till doubled in bulk, about 2 hours.

Punch the dough down, cover with plastic wrap, and refrigerate overnight.

To make the beignets, form the cheese into 2-inch balls and set aside.

(continued overleaf)

On a floured surface, roll out the chilled dough ¼ inch thick, cut into 2½-inch rounds, and arrange in small stacks.

Dust each cheese ball with flour and place on a round of dough. In a bowl, beat the eggs with the water, salt, and nutmeg and brush the edges of each round with this egg wash. Top with a second round of dough, press the edges together to seal securely, and refrigerate for 1 hour.

In a deep fryer or large, heavy saucepan, heat about 1 inch of oil to 375°F on a deep-fat thermometer, fry the beignets in batches till golden, 4 to 5 minutes, and drain on paper towels.

Serve the beignets topped with chopped capers.

 To test the temperature of fat without a deep-fat thermometer, drop a morsel of food, cube of bread, or speck of batter into the fat. When it starts bubbling and sizzling, the fat is hot enough.

Virginia Vegetable and Cheddar Supper Fry

MAKES 4 SERVINGS

Not really an omelette, a Southern "supper fry" is an egg dish that, since it is covered and fried slowly over moderately low heat, is firm but light and tender. This particular fry hails from an old college mate in Roanoke, Virginia, who was always adept at coming up with something quick and tasty for supper on dull Sunday evenings. Alan would typically serve the cheesy wedges with crisp hashed brown potatoes and spicy pickled peaches he'd put up at the end of summer.

6 tablespoons (³/₄ stick) butter
4 scallions (part of green tops included), finely chopped
1 small red bell pepper, seeded and finely chopped
¹/₂ cup finely chopped fresh mushrooms
6 large eggs
5 tablespoons milk
¹/₂ cup shredded extra-sharp cheddar cheese
Salt and freshly ground black pepper to taste

In a medium skillet, melt 3 tablespoons of the butter over moderate heat, add the scallions, bell pepper, and mushrooms, stir till the vegetables soften, about 5 minutes, and remove from the heat.

In a bowl, beat the eggs and milk till frothy, add the vegetables, cheese, and salt and pepper, and stir till well blended.

In a large, heavy skillet, melt the remaining 3 tablespoons butter over moderately low heat, add the egg mixture, cover, and let fry slowly till the eggs are almost set, lifting the mixture from time to time with a spatula and allowing the uncooked part to flow underneath. Continue to fry till the cheese is melted and the eggs firmly set, about 2 minutes.

To serve, cut the fry into wedges and serve immediately.

Meats

Natchitoches Meat Pies

MAKES ABOUT 18 SMALL PIES

I've been fascinated by these sensational fried meat pies ever since I first tasted one at James Lasyone's legendary restaurant in Natchitoches, Louisiana, back in the 1970s, and have never stopped trying to perfectly duplicate the highly guarded recipe—known only to members of the Lasyone family. The fried dough of these half-moon pies is as important as the filling, and the secret to making them as crisp and ungreasy as possible is to ensure that the temperature of the cooking oil never falls below 365°F. The stuffed, uncooked pies can be very successfully frozen in plastic bags, then thawed and fried briefly for all sorts of last-minute emergencies. Also feel free to try any meat combinations for the filling.

THE FILLING
2 tablespoons peanut or vegetable oil
¾ pound beef chuck
¾ pound ground pork
½ cup chopped scallions (part of green tops
   included)
1 garlic clove, minced
1 teaspoon salt
1 teaspoon freshly ground black pepper
¼ teaspoon cayenne pepper
2 tablespoons all-purpose flour

THE PASTRY
1 cup all-purpose flour
1 teaspoon baking powder
½ teaspoon salt
3 tablespoons vegetable shortening
1 large egg, beaten
½ cup milk

1 cup peanut oil

To make the filling, heat the oil in a large skillet over moderate heat, add the beef, pork, scallions, and garlic, and cook, stirring and breaking up the meats, till the beef loses its red color. Add the remaining ingredients and continue to cook, stirring, till the mixture is almost dry, about 10 minutes. Transfer to a bowl, let cool, then chill.

To make the pastry, sift the flour, baking powder, and salt into a bowl, add the shortening, and cut with a pastry cutter till the mixture resembles coarse cornmeal. Add the egg and milk and stir till a ball of dough forms. Transfer the dough to a lightly floured surface, roll out about ½ inch thick, and, using the lid of a coffee can, cut out rounds of dough.

To assemble the pies, place a heaping tablespoon of filling on one side of each round of dough. With your fingertips, dampen the pie edges with water, fold the other sides of dough over the filling, and seal the edges with a fork dipped in water. Prick twice with a fork on top.

To fry, heat the oil in a medium cast-iron skillet to 365°F on a deep-fat thermometer, quickly fry each pie till golden, about 3 minutes on each side, and drain briefly on paper towels. Keep warm, and serve as hot as possible.

✻ If spilled fat should ignite on the stove, use a tested fire extinguisher, baking soda, or salt to extinguish the flames—never water or flour.

Skillet Steaks with Chive Butter

MAKES 4 SERVINGS

Call it "grilled," "pan-broiled," "seared," or any other politically correct cooking technique, but in the South, any steak cooked in a skillet on top of the stove is fried—pure and simple. And when handled with care, the results are succulent and wonderful. Here garlic is used only to flavor the cooking fat and impart its essence into the meat, and the steaks are served with just enough compound chive butter to give them additional savor and juiciness. Another possibility is to discard the garlic cloves and all but a couple of tablespoons of cooking fat, deglaze the skillet with $\frac{1}{2}$ cup of red wine till slightly reduced, and spoon the sauce over the steaks. These sumptuous steaks really should never be cooked more than medium-rare.

THE CHIVE BUTTER
8 tablespoons (1 stick) butter
1 tablespoon chopped fresh chives
1 tablespoon chopped fresh parsley leaves

THE STEAKS
Four 6-ounce beef tenderloin steaks, about 2
  inches thick
Salt and crushed black pepper to taste
4 tablespoons ($\frac{1}{2}$ stick) butter
6 garlic cloves, peeled

To make the chive butter, place the butter in a bowl and beat with an electric mixer till creamy. Add the chives and parsley, stir till well blended, and chill for 15 minutes. Scrape the butter onto a large piece of plastic wrap, roll into an 8 by 2-inch log, and twist the wrap at the ends. Refrigerate at least 1 hour before using.

To fry the steaks, season each steak on both sides with salt and pepper, pressing the pepper into the meat. In a large cast-iron skillet, melt the butter over moderate heat, add the garlic cloves, and stir till softened and golden, about 10 minutes. Arrange the steaks between the garlic cloves and fry till nicely browned, about 15 minutes. Turn the steaks, fry on the other side till cooked medium-rare, 10 to 15 minutes, and transfer to warmed serving plates. Discard the garlic.

To serve, cut the chive butter into $\frac{1}{4}$-inch-thick slices, place a slice on top of each steak, and serve immediately.

Mama Dip's Pepper Steak

MAKES 6 SERVINGS

Mama Dip's restaurant in Chapel Hill, North Carolina, is renowned for classic Southern dishes that owner Mildred Council has been serving for decades, and none is more popular than this unusual "pepper steak," which is nothing like a French steak au poivre with crushed or cracked peppercorns and a creamy sauce but rather a chopped beef patty with green bell pepper and pimentos and pan gravy. Some regulars say the specialty is simply Mama Dip's unique take on Salisbury steak, but whatever the origins, it's one of the most subtle and gratifying fried dishes you'll ever taste—ideal with some hashed brown potatoes, a mess of turnip greens, and hot cornbread on the side.

¼ cup vegetable oil
1 small onion, finely chopped
½ medium green bell pepper, seeded and
    finely chopped
1½ pounds ground beef round
One 2-ounce jar pimentos, drained and finely
    chopped

1 large egg, beaten
½ cup dry bread crumbs
Salt and freshly ground black pepper to taste
1 cup plus 2 tablespoons all-purpose flour
1 cup water

In a small skillet, heat 2 tablespoons of the oil over moderate heat, add the onion and bell pepper, and stir till tender, about 5 minutes. Remove the pan from the heat and let cool.

In a bowl, combine the cooled vegetables, beef, pimentos, egg, bread crumbs, and salt and pepper, mix till well blended, and form the mixture into 6 oval patties. Dredge the patties in the 1 cup of flour to coat on both sides and set aside.

In a large, heavy skillet, heat the remaining 2 tablespoons oil over moderate heat, add the patties, and fry till golden brown, 4 to 5 minutes on each side. Transfer the patties to a plate, pour off all but 2 tablespoons of fat from the skillet, add the remaining 2 tablespoons flour, and stir till browned. Add the water and stir till the gravy thickens, about 5 minutes. Return the patties to the skillet with the gravy, turn off the heat, cover, and let stand till ready to serve.

Serve the steaks hot with gravy spooned over the tops.

Country-Fried Steak with Onion Gravy

MAKES 4 SERVINGS

O ften referred to in the Deep South as "chicken-fried steak," this steak with creamy onion gravy has been a Southern favorite for generations (especially in Texas) and can be either the worst dish imaginable or one of the most memorable, depending on the cut of meat used, how long the steak is fried, and the quality of the gravy. The only cubed (tenderized) steak I'll buy is top or bottom round, I'd never fry the steaks for more than about 2 minutes on each side for perfect moist tenderness, and not only must the gravy be flavored with a little bacon grease to taste right but it also must be whisked fairly slowly till it is properly thickened and smooth. When country-fried steak is prepared correctly, served with crispy hashed brown potatoes and a mess of peas, there's simply no better and honest dish. And if you don't believe me, ask the famous Texas gossip columnist Liz Smith, who still prides herself on the steak she's been making for friends since she was a young cowgirl.

THE STEAKS
¼ cup milk
1 large egg
1 cup dry bread crumbs
Salt and freshly ground black pepper to taste
Cayenne pepper to taste
Four 4-ounce beef cube steaks
2 tablespoons vegetable oil
2 tablespoons bacon grease

THE GRAVY
2 tablespoons bacon grease
1 large onion, minced
1 tablespoon all-purpose flour
1 cup heavy cream
1 cup milk
Salt and freshly ground black pepper to taste

To fry the steaks, combine the milk and egg in a small bowl and whisk till well blended. In another bowl, mix the bread crumbs, salt and pepper, and cayenne till well blended, and transfer the mixture to a plate. Dip each steak into the liquid, coat with bread crumbs on each side, and place on a plate.

(continued on next page)

In a large cast-iron skillet, heat the oil and bacon grease over moderately high heat till quite hot. Add 2 of the steaks to the pan, cook for about 2 minutes on each side or till golden brown, transfer to a plate, and keep warm. Repeat with the other 2 steaks and reserve the pan drippings.

To make the gravy, heat the bacon grease over moderate heat, add the onion, and cook, stirring, for about 1 minute. Sprinkle the flour over the onion and stir for 1 minute longer, scraping up any brown bits from the pan. Add the heavy cream, milk, and salt and pepper and whisk till the gravy is thickened and smooth, 6 to 7 minutes.

To serve, place the steaks on individual plates and ladle gravy over each.

 To avoid spattering or popping, all moist foods to be fried should first be patted dry with paper towels.

Chopped Steak with Caramelized Bourbon Onion Gravy

MAKES 4 SERVINGS

Once was the time when even the most deluxe steak houses in the country prided themselves as much on a well-concocted and beautifully fried chopped steak as on prized sirloins and fillets, but about the only place today where you find chopped steak (or "hamburger steak") on the menu is at more humble family restaurants in the South. That's sad, because when ground beef is blended with the right ingredients, properly seasoned, and fried to juicy perfection, nothing is more delicious and economical to prepare at home. For the gravy, fry the onions till they just caramelize but are still soft, and reduce the liquid only till it begins to thicken and coats a spoon.

1 pound ground beef round
2 scallions (part of green tops included), minced
1 garlic clove, minced
3 tablespoons minced fresh parsley leaves
1 large egg, beaten
½ teaspoon dry mustard
1 tablespoon Worcestershire sauce

Salt and freshly ground black pepper to taste
¼ cup fresh bread crumbs
2 tablespoons vegetable oil
2 tablespoons butter
1 large onion, thinly sliced
¼ cup all-purpose flour
½ cup bourbon
1½ cups beef broth

Preheat the oven to 250°F.

In a bowl, combine the beef, scallions, garlic, parsley, egg, mustard, Worcestershire, salt and pepper, and bread crumbs and mix with your hands till well blended and smooth. Shape the mixture into 4 oval patties of equal size and set aside.

In a large, heavy skillet, heat the oil over moderate heat, add the patties, and fry till browned, about 5 minutes on each side. Transfer the patties to a plate and keep warm in the oven.

Melt the butter in the skillet, reduce the heat slightly, add the onion, and stir till caramelized, 10 to 12 minutes. Sprinkle on the flour, stir well, add the bourbon, and stir, scraping up the browned bits from the bottom of the pan. Add the broth, stir till smooth, bring to a low boil, and cook till the gravy thickens, about 10 minutes.

Spoon the gravy over the steaks and serve hot.

Corned Beef Skillet Hash

MAKES 4 TO 6 SERVINGS

Never is the art of Southern frying put more to the test than in the production of corned beef hash made with leftover corned beef and served either at breakfast or, with maybe steamed asparagus or a tart green salad, for a casual Sunday supper. Great corned beef hash should be toothfully crusty on the outside with a soft, succulent interior, and one trick to ensure the right texture is to mash half the boiled potatoes before adding the coarsely chopped ones and other ingredients to the mixture to be fried. To prevent burning, remember that browning the second side of the cake usually takes less time than the first and so it should be watched carefully. While the hash is traditionally served with a poached egg on top, it's equally delicious either plain or with a few dabs of ketchup.

2 cups coarsely chopped boiled potatoes
1 small onion, minced
1 garlic clove, minced
2 cups coarsely chopped cooked corned beef
1 tablespoon minced fresh parsley leaves
1 tablespoon Dijon mustard

⅛ teaspoon grated nutmeg
Freshly ground black pepper to taste
¼ cup chicken broth
4 tablespoons (½ stick) butter
4 to 6 large poached eggs, kept warm

In a large bowl, mash half the potatoes with a sturdy fork till smooth, add the onion and garlic, and stir till well blended. Add the remaining potatoes, corned beef, parsley, mustard, nutmeg, pepper, and broth and stir till the mixture is thoroughly blended.

In a large cast-iron skillet, melt the butter over moderate heat, add the corned beef mixture, and stir till lightly browned, about 2 minutes. With a spatula, press the mixture into a flat cake and cook till browned and crusty on the bottom, about 10 minutes. Turn the cake over and cook till browned and crusty on the other side, 8 to 10 minutes. Transfer the hash to a plate, cut into wedges, and serve each wedge hot topped with a poached egg.

Rosemary Pork Chops with Caramelized Vidalia Onions

MAKES 4 SERVINGS

As every good Southern cook knows, the problem with frying any pork chops is keeping the meat juicy and tender, initial reason enough for never buying chops that are too thin and dry out almost the second they hit the pan. One trick is to cover the pan with foil during the final minutes of frying to retain as much moisture as possible. Another, as in this classic recipe, is to serve the chops with soft, caramelized onions, the best and sweetest of which are our legendary Vidalias. Here, the onions are cooked separately in case, after the chops have been fried, you might want to deglaze the pan with a little bourbon, Southern Comfort, or even orange juice to produce a tasty gravy. So long as your skillet is at least 12 inches wide, you can also just cook the onions and chops at the same time, pile the softened onions on top of the chops for the last few minutes, cover with foil, and almost guarantee meat that remains moist. Note further that a chopped apple cooked with the onions adds not only moisture but also more flavor to the dish.

---

4 tablespoons (½ stick) butter
2 Vidalia onions, sliced
1 rosemary sprig, leaves stripped

Four 1-inch-thick loin pork chops
Salt and freshly ground black pepper to taste

In a large, heavy skillet, melt 2 tablespoons of the butter over moderate heat, add the onions and rosemary leaves, and stir till the onions caramelize, about 7 minutes. Transfer to a plate and keep warm.

Season the pork chops with salt and pepper, add the remaining 2 tablespoons butter to the skillet, add the pork chops, and fry till golden brown on one side, about 8 minutes. Turn the chops, cover the pan with a piece of foil, and fry till the other side is golden brown, 6 to 7 minutes. Transfer to heated plates and serve hot with the caramelized onions.

Pork Chops with Sage and Apple Cider Gravy

MAKES 4 SERVINGS

Fried pork chops do not have to be the dry, tough disaster we encounter much too often, and one sure way to guarantee moist tenderness is to braise them in a flavorful liquid after they've been browned and serve them with a sapid pan gravy. You can also stir a few chopped apples into the gravy, or serve the chops with sautéed apples, apricots, or peaches spooned over the top. Fresh sage does make a big difference in this dish, so shop accordingly.

½ cup all-purpose flour
1 teaspoon minced fresh sage leaves
Salt and freshly ground black pepper to taste
4 pork loin chops, about ¾ inch thick

3 tablespoons butter
1½ cups apple cider
1 tablespoon chopped fresh chives

On a plate, combine the flour, sage, and salt and pepper and mix till well blended. Dredge the pork chops on both sides in the mixture and place on another plate.

In a large, heavy skillet, melt 2 tablespoons of the butter over moderate heat, add the chops, and fry on both sides till browned. Add the cider, reduce the heat to low, cover, and simmer till the chops are very tender, about 30 minutes.

Transfer the chops to a heated platter, add the remaining 1 tablespoon butter plus the chives to the liquid in the skillet, increase the heat to moderate, and reduce till the gravy is nicely thickened, about 5 minutes.

Spoon the gravy over the chops and serve hot.

Creole Picnic Chops

MAKES 4 SERVINGS

Referring to the cut of pork shoulder marketed as "fresh picnic," these succulent chops are first fried till nicely browned, then simmered slowly in the skillet with other ingredients, assertive seasonings, and just enough winey liquid to keep them moist and make them tender. The sauce should be fairly thin but not watery, so you may have to reduce it slightly just before spooning it over the chops. For this particular dish, be sure to use rib and not loin chops if you want the meat to be fork-tender, and for real Creole/Cajun flavor, be liberal with the Tabasco.

3 tablespoons peanut oil
4 rib pork chops, about ½ inch thick
1 large onion, finely chopped
1 medium green bell pepper, seeded and
  finely chopped
1 garlic clove, minced
½ cup dry white wine

One 16-ounce can crushed tomatoes with
  juice
¼ teaspoon sugar
1 tablespoon Worcestershire sauce
Tabasco sauce to taste
1 bay leaf
Salt and freshly ground black pepper to taste

In a large, deep skillet, heat half the oil over moderate heat, add the chops, and brown on both sides. Transfer the chops to a plate and discard the fat from the skillet.

Add the remaining oil to the skillet, add the onion, bell pepper, and garlic, and stir till lightly browned, about 8 minutes. Add the wine and bring to a boil, scraping browned bits from the bottom of the pan. Return the chops to the pan and spoon some of the onion and bell pepper over them. Add the tomatoes and their juice, the sugar, Worcestershire, Tabasco, bay leaf, salt and pepper, and enough water to just cover. Bring to a boil, reduce the heat to low, cover, and simmer the chops till they are very tender, about 45 minutes. If the sauce is too watery, increase the heat to high and boil down to thicken.

To serve, spoon hot sauce over each chop.

Blue Cheese–Stuffed Pork Cutlets

MAKES 4 SERVINGS

Southerners love pork (and chicken) cutlets stuffed with everything from minced ham to onion and garlic to rice and raisins, then fried to a golden brown, but never is the dish more sumptuous than when the cutlets are filled with tangy blue cheese redolent of sage and served with a tart baked apple or spicy chunky applesauce. Today you can certainly find packaged pork cutlets in most markets, but why pay extra for the convenience when it's so easy to pound loin chops (with or without the bone) for less cost and to the exact thickness you need? When shopping, do note that the chops should be about ½ inch thick.

---

4 boneless pork loin chops, about ½ pound each
Salt and freshly ground black pepper to taste
½ pound blue cheese, chilled
½ teaspoon powdered sage

½ cup all-purpose flour
2 large eggs, beaten
1 cup dry bread crumbs
Peanut oil for deep frying

On a flat surface, pound the pork chops with a mallet or heavy skillet till about ¼ inch thick and season with salt and pepper. In a bowl, combine the cheese and sage, mix well with your hands, divide into 4 equal portions, and shape each into an oval. Place an oval in the center of each pounded cutlet, bring up the edges of the cutlets to enclose the ovals envelope-style, and press the seams tightly to seal.

Dredge each cutlet in the flour, shaking off excess, dip each into the egg, and then dredge each in the bread crumbs.

In a large, heavy skillet, heat about 1½ inches of oil over moderate heat, add the cutlets, and cook till nicely browned, 6 to 7 minutes, turning as necessary. Drain briefly on paper towels and serve immediately.

Fresh Country Pork Sausage Patties

MAKES 4 SERVINGS

This is the fresh country sausage I still grind in an old manual meat grinder that I inherited from my mother, who inherited it from her mother, which is used mostly to make fried patties to go with fried eggs, grits, and the other components of a real Southern breakfast. I do not recommend grinding this sausage in a food processor, and nothing toughens the patties more than overcooking them. This recipe makes about 3 pounds of sausage meat, which, wrapped tightly in plastic wrap, freezes well for up to 2 months.

---

2 pounds boneless pork shoulder, chilled
1 pound fresh pork fat, chilled
1 tablespoon salt
2 teaspoons ground sage

1 teaspoon freshly ground black pepper
1 teaspoon crushed red pepper flakes
2 tablespoons cold water

Cut the pork and pork fat into 2-inch chunks and pass first through the coarse blade, then through the fine blade of a meat grinder into a large bowl. Add the remaining ingredients, moisten both hands with water, and knead the mixture till well blended and smooth. Wrap the sausage in plastic wrap and chill in the refrigerator for at least 2 hours before using.

With your hands, form part of the mixture into 4 patties about 4 inches in diameter and ¼ inch thick and store the remaining mixture in the refrigerator or freezer. Arrange the patties in a large, heavy skillet and fry over moderate heat till cooked through, about 8 minutes on each side. Drain on paper towels and serve hot.

Poor Man's Bacon with Milk Gravy

MAKES 4 SERVINGS

R eferred to as "poor man's bacon" throughout the state of Tennessee, fried streak-o'-lean is long strips of lean salt pork cut from pig belly, battered, fried till crisp, and served with milk gravy for breakfast or supper with grits, egg, and fried green tomatoes. Soaking the slices in buttermilk not only gives them more succulent flavor but leaches out part of the salt; thus there's no need to parboil the meat if (unlike most Southerners) you have a strong objection to salt. Do note that this gravy should be nicely thickened and slightly dark.

THE BACON
1 pound lean salt pork, rind removed
1½ cups buttermilk
1 cup cornmeal
½ teaspoon freshly ground black pepper

¼ pound (½ cup) lard

THE GRAVY
2 tablespoons all-purpose flour
2 cups whole milk

Cut the salt pork into long, ¼-inch-thick slices, place in a shallow pan or bowl, pour the buttermilk over the top, and let soak for 30 minutes.

In a shallow baking pan, combine the cornmeal and pepper, mix well, and dredge the pork slices well in the mixture. In a large cast-iron skillet, melt the lard over moderate heat, add the slices in batches, fry till golden brown and crisp, 5 to 7 minutes on each side, and drain on paper towels.

To make the gravy, pour off all but about 2 tablespoons of drippings from the skillet, add the flour, and stir over moderate heat till browned. Slowly add the milk and stir steadily till the gravy thickens slightly.

Serve the pork slices with hot milk gravy spooned over the top.

Carolina Fried Livermush

MAKES AT LEAST 6 SERVINGS

Shelby, North Carolina, lays claim to be not only one of the state's finest producers of "western-style" pork barbecue but also home of the livermush that Tar Heels love to fry for breakfast and rugged sandwiches. The town even sponsors a livermush festival every fall, and while I know that the folks in Shelby take their livermush made with pork liver and "head parts" of the pig very seriously, it's also true that I grew up in Charlotte eating either my mother's homemade version of the specialty or a commercial brand made in Greensboro that is still available all over the state and is as popular as when I was a lad. Out of state, some people feel that Carolina fried livermush is an acquired taste since the flavor is not exactly timid, but all I can say is that I've never had guests reject it when I've used my mother's rather tame recipe and served the patties with a typical Southern country breakfast. When shopping, do ask the butcher for pork liver in one piece.

1 pound fresh pork liver
1 pound fresh unsalted pork belly
1 medium onion

1 teaspoon dried sage
Salt and freshly ground black pepper to taste
Bacon grease for frying

In a large saucepan, combine the liver, pork belly, and onion and add enough water to cover. Bring to a boil, reduce the heat to low, cover, and simmer for about 2 hours.

With a slotted spoon, transfer the ingredients to a food processor, reserving the cooking liquid. Grind the ingredients coarsely. Scrape into a bowl, add the sage and salt and pepper, and mix till well blended. Form the mixture into 3- to 4-inch patties with your hands, adding just enough of the reserved cooking liquid to make the patties hold together nicely.

To fry, pour a film of bacon grease into a large cast-iron skillet over moderate heat, add half the patties, fry on both sides till golden brown, about 10 minutes in all, and drain on paper towels. Repeat with more bacon grease and the remaining patties.

Serve either as a breakfast meat or on a sandwich.

Fried Crumbed Pigs' Ears

MAKES 6 SERVINGS

Available dressed and packaged in all Southern country markets and increasingly from good butchers elsewhere, sweet, mild, gelatinous pigs' ears are never so delicious as when they are battered in buttermilk, crumbed, and deep-fried in lard to crispy perfection. Just remember that all pigs' ears must be first tenderized in simmering liquid, then weighted down till fully flattened before frying. Otherwise, they're almost guaranteed to be tough and unmanageable. Traditionally, the fried ears are served with either mustard or hot red pepper vinegar—or both—and nothing goes better with them than marinated cucumber or beet slices and a pan of hot cornbread.

6 pigs' ears, dressed and well rinsed
2 medium onions, quartered
2 celery ribs, cut into thirds
2 medium carrots, scraped and cut into thirds
2 teaspoons dried thyme
6 black peppercorns

4 whole cloves
1 bay leaf
Salt to taste
1 cup buttermilk
$\frac{1}{2}$ cup dry bread crumbs
Lard for deep frying

In a large pot or casserole, combine the pigs' ears, onions, celery, carrots, thyme, peppercorns, cloves, bay leaf, and salt, add enough water to cover, and bring to a boil, skimming any scum off the top. Reduce the heat to low, cover, and simmer till the ears are tender, 2 to 2½ hours.

Transfer the ears to a large, shallow baking pan, spoon a little clear cooking liquid over the tops, weight them down with a large, heavy pot, cover with plastic wrap, and let stand till flattened, about 2 hours.

Remove the ears from the liquid, discard the liquid, and cut the ears in half lengthwise. Dip the ears in the buttermilk, coat lightly with the bread crumbs, and place on a plate.

In a deep fryer, melt enough lard to measure about 2 inches, heat to 365°F on a deep-fat thermometer, fry the ears till golden and crispy, 5 to 7 minutes on each side, and drain on paper towels. Serve hot.

Ham Croquettes

MAKES 6 SERVINGS

As a child in North Carolina, I looked forward to nothing more when Mother would bake a big sugar-cured ham than the ham salad and ham croquettes I always knew she would make with ground or chopped leftovers, and my passion for the succulent croquettes has never faded. Some Southerners like to serve their croquettes with a mustard or tomato sauce, but since I feel a sauce distorts the wonderful crispy texture, I prefer my croquettes plain. For the very best texture, the ham mixture really should be refrigerated overnight before being formed into patties. These same croquettes can also be made with ground or chopped cooked chicken, in which case dried tarragon might be substituted for the sage.

---

4 tablespoons (½ stick) butter
3 scallions (white part only), finely chopped
3 tablespoons all-purpose flour, plus extra for dredging
1½ cups milk
4 cups coarsely chopped cooked ham

3 large egg yolks
¼ teaspoon dried sage, crumbled
Salt and freshly ground black pepper to taste
1 large egg, beaten with 2 tablespoons water
2 cups fine dry bread crumbs
Peanut oil for deep frying

In a saucepan, melt the butter over moderate heat, add the scallions and flour, and whisk till soft and well blended, about 2 minutes. Whisking rapidly, add the milk till well blended, add the ham, stir well, and remove from the heat. Whisking rapidly, add the egg yolks, return to the heat, add the sage and salt and pepper, and whisk till well blended. Scrape the mixture into a dish, cover, and refrigerate overnight.

With your hands, divide the mixture into 6 balls and roll lightly in the flour. Pat the balls into smooth oval patties, dip briefly into the egg wash, dredge in the bread crumbs, and place on a plate till ready to fry.

In a large, heavy skillet, heat about 1 inch of oil over moderately high heat for about 1 minute, fry the patties till golden brown, about 3 minutes on each side, and drain on paper towels. Serve piping hot.

Country Ham with Red-Eye Gravy

MAKES 4 SERVINGS

Fried country ham with red-eye gravy is as beloved by Southerners for breakfast or supper as the fried eggs, grits, and biscuits that are usually served with it. If the ham is properly cured, well aged, and has sufficient fat around the slices, the gravy can be made with only water to deglaze the browned bits in the skillet; otherwise, brewed coffee is needed to produce a rich flavor and sturdy texture. If the ham does not have enough fat to render, fry it in a little butter or bacon grease. As for presoaking the ham slices in water to leach out some of the salt, just remember that this dubious process also leaches out lots of authentic Southern flavor. Be warned that overcooking the ham virtually promises toughness.

---

4 slices cured country ham, about ¼ inch thick

1 teaspoon sugar
½ cup brewed coffee

Trim the fat from the edges of the ham, place the fat in a large cast-iron skillet, and fry over moderate heat till fully rendered. Discard the browned pieces of fat, add the ham slices to the skillet, fry till nicely browned, 4 to 5 minutes on each side, and transfer to a heated serving platter.

Pour off all but about 1 tablespoon of fat from the skillet, add the sugar, and stir till the sugar begins to caramelize, about 30 seconds. Add the coffee and stir steadily for about 1 minute, scraping up the browned bits on the bottom of the skillet.

Pour the hot gravy over the ham slices and serve immediately.

 Never use the same cooking fat to fry different styles of food.

Veal Cutlets with Mushrooms and Port Wine Sauce

MAKES 4 SERVINGS

Veal has never been a popular meat in Southern cookery, mainly because it has so little flavor, but when cutlets are doctored with garlic and mushrooms and served with a sturdy Port wine (or Madeira) sauce, the results can be memorable. This dish couldn't be simpler to prepare. Just take care not to toughen the cutlets by overcooking them. For a truly elegant dish with even more intense flavor, substitute shiitakes, morels, ceps, or other wild mushrooms for the more ordinary button variety.

½ cup all-purpose flour
½ teaspoon salt
¼ teaspoon freshly ground black pepper
4 veal cutlets, about 1 pound total

3 tablespoons olive oil
½ pound fresh mushrooms, sliced
1 garlic clove, minced
¼ cup Port wine

On a plate, combine the flour, salt, and pepper and stir till well blended. Dredge the cutlets on both sides in the flour and place on a plate.

In a large, heavy skillet, heat 2 tablespoons of the oil over moderate heat, add the cutlets, and cook till nicely browned, about 8 minutes on each side. Transfer the cutlets to a heated serving dish.

Add the remaining 1 tablespoon oil to the skillet, add the mushrooms and garlic, and stir till softened, about 5 minutes. Add the wine and stir well, scraping up any browned bits on the bottom of the pan, till the sauce is slightly reduced. Pour the sauce over the cutlets and serve immediately.

Craig's Delta Grillades and Grits

MAKES 6 SERVINGS

Grillades and grits, made with either veal or beef, are a popular breakfast and lunch dish throughout Louisiana and Mississippi, and while my regular Creole recipe usually involves beef round, I must say this suave version that my Mississippi friend and neighbor Craig Claiborne once prepared for me is equally delicious and ideal for a sophisticated brunch. Do not pound the veal so much that the fibers break down, and remember that the meat must be well browned to give the right dark color to the sauce.

---

1 pound boneless veal shoulder or leg, cut into 3 slices of equal thickness
1 teaspoon minced garlic (or ¼ teaspoon garlic powder)
3 tablespoons all-purpose flour
¼ teaspoon cayenne pepper
Salt and freshly ground black pepper to taste
2 tablespoons lard

1 medium onion, finely chopped
1 small green bell pepper, seeded and finely chopped
1 large ripe tomato, seeded and finely chopped
1 cup beef broth
1 cup grits, boiled according to package directions

Cut the veal slices crosswise to produce 6 pieces and pound the pieces with a mallet or rolling pin to about a ¼-inch thickness. Rub on all sides with the garlic, then sprinkle all over with the flour, cayenne, and salt and pepper.

In a large, heavy skillet, melt the lard over moderately high heat, add the veal pieces, and fry till nicely browned, about 3 minutes on each side. Transfer the meat to a plate, add the onion and bell pepper to the skillet, and stir till softened, about 3 minutes. Add the tomato, broth, and salt and pepper to taste and stir till well blended. Return the veal to the sauce, turn to coat well, cover, reduce the heat to low, and cook till the meat is very tender, 20 to 25 minutes.

To serve, either spoon the grillades over mounds of hot grits on serving plates or serve the grits on the side.

Rosemary Lamb Chops

MAKES 4 SERVINGS

Cut from the rack, succulent rib lamb chops are relished as much by Southern-ers as anyone else, and when I see the expensive chops on sale, I always grab a pound or so with the intention of coating them with garlicky rosemary bread crumbs and frying them gently just till golden and crusty and never more than medium-rare. If you like, you can also sprinkle a little fresh lemon juice over the chops for extra tang just before they're served.

½ cup fresh bread crumbs
1 teaspoon minced fresh rosemary leaves
1 garlic clove, minced
Salt and freshly ground black pepper to taste
8 rib lamb chops, trimmed of excess fat

½ cup all-purpose flour
2 large eggs, beaten
3 tablespoons butter
1 tablespoon vegetable oil

On a plate, combine the bread crumbs, rosemary, garlic, and salt and pepper, and mix till well blended.

Dredge the lamb chops in the flour, shaking off excess, dip into the eggs, dredge evenly in the bread crumb mixture, and place on a plate.

In a large, heavy skillet, melt the butter with the oil over moderate heat, add the chops, and fry gently till golden, 2 to 3 minutes. Turn the chops over, fry till golden and crisp, about 2 minutes for medium-rare, drain on paper towels, and serve hot.

Arkansas Frogs' Legs

MAKES 4 TO 6 SERVINGS

Green frogs and bullfrogs proliferate all along the Gulf Coast and have been braised, sautéed, and grilled for centuries as one of the region's great delicacies, but nowhere will you sample sweeter, more delectable frogs' legs than those that are typically battered in seasoned buttermilk and gently shallow fried. Fresh frogs' legs are still not that easy to find outside the Deep South, but the frozen ones (packaged in connecting pairs) now available in better markets are completely acceptable and usually less expensive than fresh ones. Properly fried, frogs' legs have a very subtle succulence, and since the meat dries and toughens quickly if overcooked, I do not recommend deep-frying them.

12 pairs dressed, plump frogs' legs, each pair
   tied together with twine at the first joints
1 cup all-purpose flour
Salt and freshly ground black pepper to taste

Cayenne pepper to taste
1 cup buttermilk
Vegetable oil for shallow frying
Lemon wedges

Place the frogs' legs in a large bowl with enough water to cover and refrigerate for 2 hours. Rinse the frogs' legs thoroughly and pat dry with paper towels.

In a large bowl, combine the flour, salt and pepper, and cayenne, and mix till well blended.

Dip the frogs' legs in the buttermilk, dredge on all sides in the seasoned flour, and place on a platter.

Preheat the oven to 250°F.

In a large cast-iron skillet, heat about ½ inch of oil to 350°F on a deep-fat thermometer, fry the frogs' legs in batches till golden brown, about 5 minutes on each side, and keep hot in the oven till ready to serve.

To serve, remove and discard the twine and serve the frogs' legs with lemon wedges.

Poultry and Game

Classic Southern Fried Chicken #1

MAKES 8 SERVINGS

This is the standard shallow-fried method of frying chicken that my mother and grandmother used and that I follow to this day when I choose not to deep-fry chicken. For uniformity and neatness, I always cut up my own whole chickens; I use only a deep cast-iron skillet or electric frypan; I depend on a deep-fat thermometer to ensure that the fat never drops below 365°F; I never crowd the pan with too many pieces of chicken; and I'm resolutely convinced that nothing absorbs excess fat from chicken like brown paper bags. The cooking times indicated are not fail-proof, so be sure to watch the chicken carefully to make sure it doesn't burn. The interior of fried chicken is perfectly moist and tender when the temperature reaches 170°F on an instant-read thermometer inserted into the thickest part of the piece. To prevent a soggy crust, never cover fried chicken while it drains or keep it warm in the oven.

Two 3-pound fryer chickens
Buttermilk
3 cups all-purpose flour
1 teaspoon salt

Freshly ground black pepper to taste
Vegetable shortening for shallow frying
1 tablespoon bacon grease

Cut up the chickens carefully and evenly into serving pieces, taking care to keep the skin of each piece intact, and rinse under cold running water. Place the pieces in a bowl, add enough buttermilk to just cover, and let soak for about 30 minutes.

In a heavy brown paper bag, combine the flour, salt, and pepper and shake till well blended. Add the chicken pieces to the bag, shake vigorously to coat evenly, tap excess flour off each piece back into the bag, and stack the pieces on a large plate.

Heat about 1½ inches of shortening in a large cast-iron skillet to 365°F on a deep-fat thermometer, or heat the fat in an electric frypan to 365°F, and add the bacon grease. Arrange the dark-meat pieces of chicken in the fat, making sure not to overcrowd the pan. Fry the chicken till golden brown and crisp, 12 to 15 minutes, turn with tongs, and fry till golden brown, about 12 minutes longer. (Turn the chicken only once.) Drain on a wire rack or another brown paper bag and repeat the procedure with the remaining chicken pieces.

Transfer the chicken to a large serving platter. Do not cover to keep warm. Serve warm or at room temperature.

Classic Southern Fried Chicken #2

MAKES 8 SERVINGS

This is my deep-fried version of fried chicken, and it was a revelation when my friend, colleague, and fellow Tar Heel Jean Anderson informed me that nothing produces a crisper crust on deep-fried chicken than self-rising flour containing a little baking powder, which reacts with the acid in the buttermilk to lighten the batter. The lard also contributes to the crunchy texture of the chicken, so do not substitute another fat. Some Southerners cover the pot and deep-fry the chicken longer at a lower temperature, but I find this can make the skin too greasy. In any case, do watch the chicken carefully once it's been turned to make sure it doesn't burn in the least, and remember that covering any fried chicken to keep it warm almost guarantees a soggy crust.

Two 3-pound fryer chickens
Buttermilk
2 cups self-rising flour
1 teaspoon salt

½ teaspoon freshly ground black pepper
⅛ teaspoon cayenne pepper
Lard for deep frying
1 tablespoon bacon grease

Cut up the chickens carefully and evenly into serving pieces, taking care to keep the skin of each piece intact, and rinse under cold running water.

Place the pieces in a bowl, add enough buttermilk to just cover, and let soak for 30 minutes to 1 hour.

In a heavy brown paper bag, combine the flour, salt, black pepper, and cayenne and shake till well blended. Add the chicken pieces to the bag, shake vigorously to coat evenly, and stack the pieces on a large plate.

In a large, heavy Dutch oven or casserole, heat about 3 inches of melted lard to 365°F on a deep-fat thermometer and add the bacon grease. Arrange the dark-meat pieces of chicken in the fat, making sure not to overcrowd the pot or allow the temperature of the fat to drop below 365°F, and fry till golden brown and crisp, 12 to 15 minutes. Turn with tongs, fry till golden brown and crisp, about 15 minutes, and drain on a wire rack or another brown paper bag. Repeat with the remaining chicken pieces.

Transfer the chicken to a large serving platter and serve warm or at room temperature.

Mississippi Honey-Battered Fried Chicken

MAKES 4 TO 6 SERVINGS

The renowned food writer and my friend and neighbor Craig Claiborne was the one who introduced me to the unusual honey-battered version of Southern fried chicken served all over his native Mississippi, and I must say it's some of the most delectable chicken you'll ever sink teeth into. To intensify the flavors, you can first marinate the chicken pieces for about an hour in the honey and vinegar, as Craig liked to do, before dredging them in the seasoned flours, but I personally prefer to mix up a tangy-sweet batter and let it meld as indicated here. If you want your fried chicken to remain crisp, remember never to cover it or keep it warm in the oven.

½ cup all-purpose flour
2 tablespoons whole-wheat flour
½ teaspoon salt
Freshly ground black pepper to taste
½ cup honey

3 tablespoons fruit-flavored vinegar
½ cup lard
½ cup peanut oil
One 3½-pound chicken, cut into serving
   pieces

In a bowl, combine the two flours, salt, pepper, honey, and vinegar, stir till well blended, and let the batter stand for 1 hour.

In a large cast-iron skillet or electric frypan, add the lard and peanut oil and heat to 365°F on a deep-fat thermometer. Stir the batter again, dip the dark-meat pieces of chicken into the batter to lightly coat, and fry in the fat till golden and crisp, 12 to 15 minutes on each side, turning once with tongs. Drain on paper towels, then repeat the procedure with the remaining chicken pieces. Do not cover to keep warm. Serve the chicken warm or at room temperature.

Maryland Fried Chicken with Cream Gravy

MAKES 4 TO 6 SERVINGS

Maryland fried chicken is technically not really "fried chicken," since the pieces are just lightly browned before being covered, simmered in liquid, and always served covered with a cream gravy. Nobody knows how the dish evolved, and arguments can become heated as to whether the gravy should be made with milk, whole cream, half-and-half, or even buttermilk. Whatever the origins and various cooking techniques, however, Maryland fried chicken is one of the true glories of Southern cooking, and when it's prepared with care, it's a dish worthy of the most sophisticated tables. Traditionally, the chicken should be served with Maryland beaten biscuits to sop up part of the gravy.

---

1 cup plus 1 tablespoon all-purpose flour
1 teaspoon salt
¼ teaspoon freshly ground black pepper
¼ teaspoon cayenne pepper
1 cup whole milk

One 3½-pound chicken, cut into serving pieces
Vegetable oil for frying
½ cup water
1 cup half-and-half

In a brown paper bag, combine 1 cup of the flour, salt, black pepper, and cayenne and shake until well blended. Pour the milk into a shallow bowl, dip the chicken pieces in the milk, then shake them in the paper bag to coat evenly, tapping off excess flour.

In a large, heavy skillet, heat about ½ inch of oil over moderately high heat, add the chicken, cover, and fry till golden, about 5 minutes on each side, turning with tongs. Uncover and continue to fry till the pieces are slightly browned all over. Pour off the fat, add the water, reduce the heat to moderate, cover, and cook till tender, 15 to 20 minutes. Transfer the chicken to a platter and keep warm.

Pour off all but 1 tablespoon of liquid from the skillet, reduce the heat to low, add the remaining 1 tablespoon flour, and stir for 3 minutes. Add the half-and-half, increase the heat to moderate, and cook till the gravy is thickened, scraping up any browned bits from the pan. Remove from the heat.

Strain the gravy over the chicken and serve immediately.

Oriental Chicken Drumettes

MAKES 6 SERVINGS

Relished in the South for their tender, sweet meat, humble chicken wings are prepared every way imaginable. When I want to serve them as a first course or cocktail appetizer, I'm prone to roll the drumsticks in Parmesan cheese and bake them till just lightly browned, but for a main course, nothing is better than crispy fried "Oriental" drumettes served with any bottled sweet chili sauce. Unlike the baked version, these must be served as piping hot as possible, and remember that overcooking the wings will only toughen and dry them out.

¼ cup soy sauce
2 tablespoons olive oil
1 tablespoon fresh lemon juice
½ teaspoon onion powder
½ teaspoon garlic powder

½ teaspoon freshly ground black pepper
3 pounds chicken wings
1 cup all-purpose flour
Peanut oil for deep frying

In a large bowl, combine the soy sauce, olive oil, lemon juice, onion powder, garlic powder, and pepper, whisk till well blended, and set the marinade aside.

Remove the tips and first joint from the chicken wings and either discard or reserve to make stock in the future. Add the drumsticks (drumettes) to the marinade, toss well, cover with plastic wrap, and refrigerate for several hours, turning once.

Place the flour in a paper or plastic bag, add the drumettes in batches, shake well to coat, and place on a large plate.

In a deep, heavy skillet, heat about 2 inches of oil to 365°F on a deep-fat thermometer, fry the drumettes in batches till golden brown, 6 to 8 minutes, turning once, and drain on paper towels. Serve hot.

 Contrary to popular opinion, if fried chicken no longer sizzles in the hot fat, it doesn't mean that the chicken is done but rather that it is overcooked and dried out.

S & W Chicken Croquettes

MAKES 6 TO 8 SERVINGS

When I was a child in Charlotte, North Carolina, it was always a treat to be taken downtown to the S & W cafeteria and choose from the vast array of Southern dishes on the lavish steam table. To be sure, there was meat loaf and barbecue and fried shrimp and roast turkey, but what I really loved was the golden chicken croquettes that were crispy and so moist and tender on the inside that they almost melted in your mouth. I figure that my mother must have somehow gotten the recipe, for the glorious croquettes that she eventually began making at home had the exact same texture and flavor as those at the S & W, and these are the croquettes that I continue to fry up to this day—usually with no adornment but sometimes with a creamy mushroom or spicy tomato sauce. Obviously, ground cooked turkey can be substituted for the chicken with equally succulent results.

---

3 tablespoons butter
1 small onion, minced
3 tablespoons all-purpose flour, plus more for dredging
½ cup chicken broth
½ cup whole milk
3 cups coarsely ground cooked chicken

¼ teaspoon grated nutmeg
Salt and freshly ground black pepper to taste
Tabasco sauce to taste
2 large egg yolks
1½ cups fine, fresh bread crumbs
1 large egg beaten with 3 tablespoons water
Vegetable oil for deep frying

In a large saucepan, melt the butter over moderate heat, add the onion, sprinkle on the 3 tablespoons flour, and whisk till softened, about 3 minutes. Whisking rapidly, add the chicken broth and milk and whisk till well blended. Add the chicken, nutmeg, salt and pepper, and Tabasco and stir till well blended. Remove the pan from the heat and, whisking constantly, add the egg yolks and whisk till well blended. Return the pan to the heat, cook, stirring, for about 2 minutes, and remove from the heat. Transfer the mixture to a bowl, let cool, then refrigerate for about 30 minutes.

Spread the flour for dredging and the bread crumbs on two separate plates. Shape the chicken mixture into 6 to 8 balls, roll lightly in the flour, and pat into oval patties. Dip the patties in the egg wash, then in the bread crumbs. Place on a large plate, cover with plastic wrap, and chill about 30 minutes before frying.

In a large, heavy skillet, heat about 1 inch of oil to 365°F on a deep-fat thermometer, add half the patties, fry till golden brown and crispy, about 3 minutes on each side, and drain on paper towels. Repeat with the remaining patties. Serve hot.

＊ For the crunchiest results in frying, batter foods by dusting them first in all-purpose flour, dipping them in an egg wash, then dredging them in bread crumbs or cornmeal.

Smothered Chicken with Artichoke Hearts

MAKES 4 TO 6 SERVINGS

Smothered chicken dishes abound all over the South, using a technique whereby a split chicken is opened up as if for broiling, fried over low heat in an iron skillet with several weights on top, then cooked further in a seasoned gravy with anything from onions to mushrooms to artichoke hearts till fork-tender. The trick, of course, is never to allow the chicken to burn, so watch it carefully and adjust the heat accordingly if necessary. Frozen or canned artichoke hearts are perfectly acceptable for this dish, and for weights, I use several canned goods or a small cast-iron skillet.

One 3½-pound chicken, split down the backbone with the breast left unsplit
Salt and freshly ground black pepper to taste
4 tablespoons (½ stick) butter
8 to 10 cooked artichoke hearts (fresh, frozen,
   or canned), cut into pieces
½ cup dry white wine

½ cup chicken broth
1 bay leaf
¼ teaspoon dried thyme, crumbled
2 garlic cloves, finely chopped
2 tablespoons finely chopped fresh parsley
   leaves

Season the chicken with the salt and pepper and fold the wings under to hold them secure.

In a large cast-iron skillet, melt 2 tablespoons of the butter over low heat, add the chicken, skin side down, cover firmly with a heavy plate that fits inside the skillet, and add several weights (such as canned goods) on top of the plate. Cook for 20 to 25 minutes, pour off most of the fat from the skillet, and add the 2 remaining tablespoons butter. Turn the chicken skin side up and scatter the artichoke hearts over and around the chicken. Add the wine, broth, bay leaf, thyme, and garlic, replace the plate and weights on top, and continue cooking over low heat till the chicken is very tender, 25 to 30 minutes.

Transfer the chicken to a warm platter and spoon the artichoke hearts over the top. Cook the liquid in the skillet until reduced by half, pour over the chicken and artichoke hearts, and sprinkle the parsley on top. Serve hot.

Chicken Dijon

MAKES 4 SERVINGS

Any dish with mustard deemed exotic in the South today is likely to be tagged "Dijon," and these delectable fried chicken breasts are one of the simplest and easiest preparations. For additional flavor, you can always enhance the two frying fats with about a tablespoon of bacon grease, and if you love mustard as much as Southerners do, by all means double the amount called for in the sauce. Just be sure to use only Dijon-style mustard and not that ghastly ballpark abomination. You might also like to sprinkle a few toasted almonds over the top of these breasts.

4 boneless, skinless chicken breast halves
Salt and freshly ground black pepper to taste
2 tablespoons butter
2 tablespoons peanut oil

2 tablespoons all-purpose flour
1 cup chicken broth
½ cup half-and-half
1 tablespoon Dijon mustard

Season the chicken breasts with salt and pepper. In a large, heavy skillet, melt the butter over moderate heat and add the oil. Add the chicken breasts, fry till golden brown, about 10 minutes on each side, and transfer to a heated serving platter.

Sprinkle the flour over the drippings in the pan and stir for 1 minute. Add the broth and half-and-half and stir till slightly thickened and smooth, about 10 minutes. Add the mustard, stir till well incorporated into the sauce, and spoon the hot sauce over the chicken breasts. Serve hot.

Country Captain Chicken

T his American classic originated in the South and is said to have been brought back to Virginia from India by a Colonial Navy captain. It's also argued that the name might be merely a corruption of the word "capon." Whatever the curried dish's history, just remember that the chicken in a genuine country captain must be initially fried before it is slowly simmered long enough for the various flavors to meld. If the juices from the tomatoes do not provide enough liquid to partly cover the chicken once it's been returned to the skillet, add about ½ cup of chicken broth. The chicken can be served either by itself or over mounds of boiled rice.

½ cup all-purpose flour
Salt and freshly ground black pepper to taste
One 3-pound chicken, cut into serving pieces
4 tablespoons (½ stick) butter
2 tablespoons vegetable oil
1 small onion, finely diced
½ small green bell pepper, seeded and finely
  diced

1 garlic clove, minced
1½ teaspoons curry powder
½ teaspoon dried thyme, crumbled
2 cups crushed canned tomatoes with juice
3 tablespoons seedless dark raisins
½ cup chopped toasted almonds

On a plate, combine the flour and salt and pepper and stir till well blended. Dredge the chicken pieces in the seasoned flour and place on another plate.

In a large, heavy skillet, melt the butter over moderate heat, add the oil, and fry the chicken on all sides till nicely browned, about 15 minutes in all. Remove the chicken from the skillet, add the onion, bell pepper, and garlic, and stir till softened, about 3 minutes. Add the curry powder, thyme, and tomatoes with their juice and stir till well blended. Return the chicken to the skillet, cover, reduce the heat to low, and cook till tender, about 20 minutes. Add the raisins, stir, and cook for 10 minutes longer.

Serve the chicken sprinkled with the almonds.

Skillet Parmesan Chicken Hash

MAKES 4 SERVINGS

Nothing illustrates the Southern art of careful frying more than a well-made skillet hash, and this one prepared with finely diced cooked chicken is one of the most popular. Leftover cooked turkey, of course, can also be used, and to give further dimension to the dish, I sometimes add a few diced olives to the chicken mixture or substitute a little curry powder for the cheese. As with any great hash, the exterior of this one should be crusty, while the interior should remain soft and moist. For a more elegant presentation, serve the portions of hash topped with poached eggs sprinkled with paprika.

2 tablespoons bacon grease
1 medium onion, minced
½ small green bell pepper, seeded and
  minced
1 garlic clove, minced
2 cups finely diced cooked chicken

2 cups cooked mashed potatoes
¼ cup grated Parmesan cheese
1 tablespoon minced fresh parsley leaves
¼ teaspoon minced fresh tarragon leaves
Salt and freshly ground black pepper to taste

In a large skillet, heat the bacon grease over moderate heat, add the onion, bell pepper, and garlic, and stir till softened, about 8 minutes. Add the chicken and potatoes and stir for 5 minutes longer. Add the cheese, parsley, tarragon, and salt and pepper and stir till well blended. Using a heavy spatula, press the mixture down and let it cook till a brown crust forms on the bottom, about 10 minutes. Using two heavy spatulas, carefully flip the hash over in the skillet and cook till the other side is crusted, 8 to 10 minutes.

Slide the hash onto a plate, cut into 4 portions, and serve immediately.

 One ounce of bacon fat has less saturated fat, cholesterol, and sodium than 1 ounce of butter.

Sherried Chicken Livers with Onions and Mushrooms

MAKES 4 TO 6 SERVINGS

These tender chicken livers are perfect for a last-minute supper or even a stylish luncheon, but whatever the occasion, by no means overcook the livers (they should remain pink on the inside). For a heartier dish, you can also add about ½ cup of sour cream with or without the sherry and serve the livers, onions, and mushrooms over boiled rice.

½ cup all-purpose flour
Salt and freshly ground black pepper to taste
1½ pounds chicken livers, trimmed of fat and
   cut in half
3 to 4 tablespoons bacon grease

4 tablespoons (½ stick) butter
1 small onion, finely chopped
¾ cup chopped fresh mushrooms
3 tablespoons sherry
Buttered toast triangles

On a plate, mix together the flour and salt and pepper and dredge the livers in the mixture, shaking off excess flour.

In a large, heavy skillet, heat the bacon grease over moderate heat, add the livers, fry till browned all over, about 5 minutes, and transfer to a plate.

Melt the butter in the skillet, add the onion and mushrooms, and stir till softened, about 3 minutes. Return the livers to the skillet, add the sherry, and stir gently for about 3 minutes.

To serve, arrange toast triangles on serving plates and spoon the hot livers, onions, and mushrooms over the top.

Lowcountry Turkey Hash Cakes

MAKES 4 TO 6 SERVINGS

Inspired by a curried turkey hash I was once served in the coastal Carolina Low-country, I came up with these fried cakes years ago and have never stopped experimenting with them. They're a perfect solution to leftover turkey during the holidays, and any time I see turkey parts on sale in the market, I always think about boiling or baking them to be used for these crusty, delectable cakes. Other ingredients that can be added to the ground turkey and vegetable mixture are minced capers, olives, crumbled fried bacon, and any number of herbs or spices. The cakes do not absorb much fat during the frying, so there's no need to lose the wonderful buttery flavor by draining them.

2 medium boiling potatoes, peeled, boiled till very tender, and coarsely chopped
8 tablespoons (1 stick) butter, at room temperature
3 cups chopped cooked turkey
1 medium onion, chopped
1 celery rib, chopped
½ green bell pepper, seeded and shopped

3 large eggs, 2 beaten
½ cup heavy cream
1½ teaspoons salt
Freshly ground black pepper to taste
1 teaspoon curry powder
¾ cup all-purpose flour
2 cups fine, dry bread crumbs
2 tablespoons vegetable oil

In a bowl, mash the potatoes to a puree with a potato masher or fork, add 4 tablespoons of the butter in pieces, and beat with a wooden spoon or electric mixer till smooth and the butter is completely absorbed.

In a blender or food processor, grind the turkey, onions, celery, and bell pepper to a medium texture and transfer to the bowl with the potatoes. Add the whole egg and stir till well blended. Add the cream, salt, pepper, and curry powder and beat till the mixture is smooth. Cover the bowl with plastic wrap and chill for 30 minutes to firm up the texture and allow the flavors to develop.

Shape the hash into 4 to 6 cakes, dust each evenly in the flour, dip in the beaten eggs, roll in the bread crumbs, and chill for 30 minutes.

In a large, heavy skillet, heat the remaining 4 tablespoons butter with the oil over moderate heat, add the cakes, and fry on both sides till golden brown and crusty, about 10 minutes in all. Serve hot.

Cajun Deep-Fried Whole Turkey

MAKES AT LEAST 8 SERVINGS

Developed some decades ago by Louisiana Cajun chefs, deep-fried turkey has taken America by storm and adds a whole new dimension to the art of Southern frying. I've never tried the method with a turkey weighing more than about 10 pounds, so if your bird is considerably larger (and you have a large enough pot to hold it easily), you will have to adjust the frying time to about an hour. In any case, the result should be a turkey that is crunchy crisp on the outside with a succulent moist interior. Only an oil such as peanut with a high smoking point should be used, and because of spattering, the oil level should be no higher than about 7 inches from the top of the pot. This turkey cannot be stuffed, so if you want to also serve dressing, it will have to be baked in the oven. Is the fried turkey really as glorious as they say? You bet it is.

One 9- to 10-pound dressed turkey (fresh or
   thawed frozen)

¼ cup Cajun-style dry seasoning (available in
   most markets)
8 quarts peanut oil

Remove the neck and giblet bag from the turkey cavity and reserve to make oven-baked dressing and/or giblet gravy. Secure the turkey legs and wings with twine and pierce the turkey all over with a fork. Season the bird inside and out with the Cajun seasoning.

In a large, heavy stockpot, heat enough oil to reach halfway up the sides to 350°F on a deep-fat thermometer. Using long-handled tongs, carefully lower the turkey into the hot oil breast side down till completely submerged and fry for about 20 minutes, maintaining the oil temperature at 350°F. Carefully turn the turkey over and fry breast side up till golden brown all over, about 15 minutes longer or till an instant-read thermometer inserted at the thickest part of the breast registers 180°F.

Carefully transfer the turkey to a heavy baking pan lined with paper towels to drain, remove the twine, and let stand for about 10 minutes before carving. Serve hot.

Turkey Scallopini with Bell Peppers and Garlic

MAKES 6 SERVINGS

If you can find prepared turkey cutlets in the market, they are ideal for these tasty scallopini. Otherwise, look for a 2-pound packaged boneless turkey breast, or use 2 large boneless chicken breast halves. Do be careful not to pound the sliced cutlets to less than about $\frac{1}{4}$ inch thick so they will hold their form when fried, and do not overcook the scallopini.

One 2-pound boneless turkey breast
$\frac{1}{2}$ cup all-purpose flour
Salt and freshly ground black pepper to taste
4 tablespoons ($\frac{1}{2}$ stick) butter
2 tablespoons olive oil
1 small green bell pepper, seeded and cut into $\frac{1}{2}$-inch-wide strips

1 small red bell pepper, seeded and cut into $\frac{1}{2}$-inch-wide strips
1 garlic clove, minced
$\frac{1}{4}$ cup dry red wine
2 tablespoons red wine vinegar

Slice the turkey breast against the grain into 6 cutlets and pound each cutlet with a mallet or rolling pin to a $\frac{1}{4}$-inch-thick scallopini. On a plate, mix the flour and salt and pepper, dredge each scallopini in the flour mixture, shaking off excess flour, and set aside.

In a large, heavy skillet, heat half the butter and oil over moderate heat, add 3 of the scallopini, fry till golden brown, 4 to 5 minutes on each side, and transfer to a heated serving platter. Repeat with the remaining butter, oil, and scallopini.

Add both bell peppers and the garlic to the skillet and stir till softened, about 3 minutes. Add the wine and vinegar, simmer for about 2 minutes longer, spoon the peppers and sauce over the turkey, and serve immediately.

Fried Stuffed Quail

MAKES 4 SERVINGS

Although small and delicate, quail can be stuffed with anything from a force-meat of cooked ham, salt pork, or sausage to a mixture of ground beef, pork, and veal to minced wild mushrooms, then tied securely with twine, shallow-fried to golden succulence, and served elegantly with wild rice at any formal Southern dinner. Do be careful when separating the fragile skin from the breasts, and don't feel that you necessarily must use up all the stuffing if it seems to be oozing too much from the cavities. As for serving, allow 2 quail per person.

¼ cup ground cooked smoked ham
2 garlic cloves, minced
2 tablespoons minced carrot
2 tablespoons minced celery
1 teaspoon dried sage, crumbled
1 teaspoon dried thyme, crumbled
1 tablespoon minced fresh parsley leaves

2 tablespoons dry bread crumbs
Salt and finely ground black pepper to taste
8 dressed quail (fresh or thawed frozen), split
  down the backbone
Peanut oil for shallow frying
2 tablespoons bacon grease

In a bowl, combine the ham, garlic, carrot, celery, herbs, parsley, bread crumbs, and salt and pepper and mash the stuffing almost to a paste. Gently separate the skin from the breasts of the quail and work some of the stuffing between the two. Pack stuffing between the thighs and breast and into any other cavities, then tie the quail with twine as tightly as possible to secure the stuffing.

In a large, heavy skillet, heat about 1 inch of oil plus the bacon grease over moderately high heat, add the quail, and fry till golden brown, about 10 minutes, turning once. Do not overcook.

Carefully remove the twine and serve the quail hot.

Hoppin' John's Fried Quail with Sausage and Oyster Cream

MAKES 4 SERVINGS

L eave it to one of the real experts of Carolina Lowcountry cooking, "Hoppin' John" Taylor, to come up with an elaborate version of fried quail that would be appropriate for the most sophisticated Southern table. I've adapted Hoppin' John's recipe to my own method of shallow-frying the quail (or, in local parlance, "partridges"), but there's no way to improve on this luscious sauce that transforms the dish into such a masterpiece. Ideally, fresh quail should be used, but frozen ones (most of which are raised on game bird farms) are almost as delicate and flavorful. As always, allow 2 quail per person.

½ pound fresh country sausage (see page 95) or commercial bulk pork sausage
1½ cups half-and-half
2 cups shucked fresh oysters, with their liquor

1 cup all-purpose flour
Salt and freshly ground black pepper to taste
8 dressed quail (fresh or thawed frozen)
Lard for shallow frying

In a heavy saucepan, break up the sausage and cook over moderate heat till all the grease is rendered and the meat evenly browned. Drain the sausage on paper towels and discard the grease from the pan.

Add the half-and-half and oyster liquor to the pan, increase the heat slightly, and reduce till just thickened, stirring and scraping up browned bits from the bottom of the pan. Reduce the heat to low, add the sausage to the cream, and stir. Add the oysters and stir just till they begin to curl, 1 to 2 minutes. Cover the sauce and keep warm.

On a plate, mix the flour and salt and pepper, and dust the quail in the seasoned flour. In a large, heavy skillet, melt about ½ inch of lard over moderately high heat, add the quail, and fry till golden brown, about 10 minutes, turning once.

To serve, transfer the quail to a heated deep platter and pour the hot sauce over the top.

Plantation Pheasant with Chanterelles and Sherry Sauce

MAKES 4 SERVINGS

During the plantation era in the South, wild pheasants were plentiful on the vast estates and, roasted over open fires, were considered ceremonial birds at lavish dinners. I'm lucky to know a couple of hunters who keep me pretty well supplied with fresh pheasants in season, but generally today most pheasants are raised in captivity for greater tenderness and marketed frozen. While frozen pheasant does not have the slightly gamy succulence of fresh and tends to have drier meat, it is nonetheless a superbly flavored bird that, when fried, resembles full-flavored, free-range chicken. Some Southern cooks like to simmer the fried pheasant briefly in liquid to ensure moistness, but so long as you don't overcook the pieces, this is not necessary.

Two 2½-pound plump, dressed pheasants (fresh or thawed frozen)
Salt and freshly ground black pepper to taste
6 tablespoons (¾ stick) butter
6 tablespoons vegetable oil

3 scallions (white part only), chopped
½ pound fresh chanterelle mushrooms
1 cup semisweet sherry
¼ cup chopped fresh parsley leaves

Cut the pheasants into serving pieces and season with salt and pepper.

In a large, heavy skillet, melt the butter over moderate heat and add the oil. Add the pheasant pieces, reduce the heat to low, and fry till golden on all sides, about 20 minutes. Transfer the pieces to a heated platter, add the scallions and mushrooms to the skillet, and stir till softened and tender, about 8 minutes. Add the sherry, increase the heat to moderate, and reduce the sherry by half. Add the parsley, stir for about 3 minutes longer, spoon the sauce over the pheasant, and serve immediately.

Fried Rabbit with Olives and Herb Wine Sauce

MAKES 4 TO 6 SERVINGS

Unlike in the rest of the country, rabbit has always played an important role in Southern cookery, and one of my earliest memories as a child in North Carolina was the sight of a neighbor bringing Mother a brace of freshly dressed wild rabbits he'd caught in some of his traps. By far the most popular preparation is buttermilk-battered rabbit simply fried in lard, but when I want to elevate the dish and keep the meat moist, as in this recipe, I simmer the browned rabbit with olives and flavorings in a sauce based on Port, Madeira, sweet vermouth, or just an ordinary red wine. Frozen dressed rabbit is now available in more and more of the finer markets, but since rabbits can be scrawny, do try to select ones with as much meat on the bones as possible.

Two 2-pound rabbits, dressed and cut into
    serving pieces
Salt and freshly ground black pepper to taste
4 tablespoons (½ stick) butter
1 tablespoon vegetable oil
1 cup semidry red wine

1 medium ripe tomato
2 garlic cloves, minced
½ teaspoon dried thyme, crumbled
½ teaspoon dried rosemary, crumbled
1 cup pitted black olives, drained

Season the rabbit pieces with salt and pepper and set aside.

In a large, deep stainless steel or enameled skillet, melt the butter over moderately high heat and add the oil. Add the rabbit pieces and fry on all sides till nicely browned, about 10 minutes. Add the wine, tomato, garlic, thyme, rosemary, and olives, reduce the heat to low, cover, and cook till the rabbit is tender and the sauce slightly thickened, 15 to 20 minutes. Taste the sauce for salt and pepper, transfer the rabbit to a heated platter, spoon the sauce over the top, and serve hot.

Venison Burgers with Sour Cream Sauce

MAKES 4 SERVINGS

Since deer hunting has always been a popular sport in the South, fresh venison is generally more available than in other areas of the country. This does not mean, however, that even most Southern cooks today don't have to settle for frozen venison steaks or stew meat when there's not a good butcher to deal with loins, racks, and saddles and grind the meat from shoulders, necks, and shanks. One type of venison that is more and more popular and easier to find is buffalo, but even ground buffalo (which tastes a lot like ground beef) is much too lean and dry to stand on its own and needs additional fat for moisture and true succulence. Any form of ground venison makes superb burgers, and when they're served with a tangy sour cream sauce, like this one, the result is memorable. Don't cook these burgers more than medium-rare for ultimate flavor and texture.

---

1 pound ground venison
½ pound ground pork fat
¼ cup all-purpose flour
Salt and freshly ground black pepper to taste
3 tablespoons butter

1 tablespoon bacon grease
1 cup beef broth
½ cup sour cream
2 tablespoons minced fresh chives

In a bowl, combine the venison and pork fat, mix with your hands till well blended, and form the mixture into 4 plump patties. On a plate, mix the flour and salt and pepper and dredge both sides of the patties lightly in the mixture.

In a large, heavy skillet, melt the butter with the bacon grease over moderate heat, add the patties, fry till nicely browned, about 8 minutes on each side, and transfer to a heated platter.

Add the broth to the skillet and stir till slightly reduced, about 5 minutes, scraping up any browned bits on the bottom of the pan. Add the sour cream and chives, stir till the sauce is slightly thickened and smooth, and pour over the patties. Serve hot.

Seafood

Fried Flounder with Pecan-Butter Sauce

MAKES 6 SERVINGS

No fish is more popular in the South than fried fillet of flounder (elsewhere it is almost always either broiled or grilled), and there are Rebs who evaluate a cook's talent solely on his or her ability to produce fried flounder that is perfectly crisp on the outside and still moist and succulent inside—no easy feat. Fried flounder with only lemon juice and maybe a sprinkling of minced fresh parsley is hard to beat on a daily basis, but if you really want to impress guests, serve the fish with this easy but sublime pecan-butter sauce—along maybe with a few extra chopped pecans scattered over the top.

THE SAUCE
4 tablespoons (½ stick) butter
½ cup coarsely chopped toasted pecans
1 scallion (part of green tops included), chopped
1 garlic clove, minced
1 teaspoon fresh lemon juice

THE FLOUNDER
½ cup milk
1 large egg, beaten
1 cup all-purpose flour
Salt and freshly ground black pepper to taste
Cayenne pepper to taste
Vegetable oil for shallow frying
6 fresh flounder fillets (about 4 ounces each)

To make the sauce, combine all the ingredients in a blender or food processor, process till creamy and smooth, 2 to 3 minutes, and set aside.

To fry the flounder, combine the milk and egg in a bowl and whisk till well blended. On a plate, combine the flour, salt and pepper, and cayenne and mix till well blended.

In a large, heavy skillet, heat about 1 inch of oil to 365°F on a deep-fat thermometer. Dip the fillets in the milk mixture, dredge in the seasoned flour, fry in the oil till golden brown, 2 to 3 minutes on each side, and drain on paper towels.

To serve, spread 2 to 3 tablespoons of the sauce over each fillet and serve immediately.

Cornmeal Porgies

MAKES 3 OR 4 SERVINGS

In the South, lean, delicate, mild porgies are also known as sea bream. They are always sold whole in markets, and one of the most popular and distinctive ways to cook them is brushed with mayonnaise, battered in seasoned cornmeal, and deep-fried till golden and crisp. This is also the way I cook spots, whiting, croakers, and any other small, firm fish I pull in on the Carolina coast. Let it be known that fried porgies are just as delicious for breakfast as at any other meal. If you've never learned to dress your own fish, this is a good time to start.

---

6 to 8 small to medium fresh porgies
½ cup yellow cornmeal
1 tablespoon commercial dried seafood seasoning

Salt and freshly ground black pepper to taste
½ cup mayonnaise
Peanut oil for deep frying
Lemon wedges

Gut the porgies, remove the heads and fins (or have the job done at the fish market), and set aside.

In a brown paper bag, combine the cornmeal, seafood seasoning, and salt and pepper and shake till well blended.

Brush both sides of the dressed fish with the mayonnaise, place in the paper bag, shake till the fish are well coated, and place on a plate.

In a deep fryer or large cast-iron skillet, heat 2 to 3 inches of oil to 365°F on a deep-fat thermometer, add half of the porgies, fry till golden brown, 2 to 3 minutes on each side, and drain on paper towels. Repeat with the remaining fish and serve immediately with lemon wedges.

 When cooking fats maintain a temperature of at least 365°F, virtually no fat is absorbed into the food.

Blackened Fish

MAKES 4 SERVINGS

I ndigenous to Louisiana, redfish has been fried in blazing-hot cast-iron skillets ("blackened") for centuries, but it was only in the 1980s that the famous Cajun chef Paul Prudhomme popularized the technique at his restaurant in New Orleans. Ever since, blackened fish has been trendy and often abused from coast to coast, which is sad since, when executed correctly, the dish not only illustrates further the fine art of Southern frying but also can produce some of the most succulent fish imaginable. It's highly unlikely you'll find redfish (even frozen) outside Louisiana, but good substitutes are red snapper, sea bass, tilefish, and grouper. Be warned that frying fish in this manner creates lots of smoke, so if you can get a cast-iron skillet extremely hot outside over an open fire or on a grill, so much the better.

3 teaspoons salt
2 teaspoons medium-hot paprika
$\frac{1}{2}$ teaspoon cayenne pepper
$\frac{1}{4}$ teaspoon freshly ground black pepper
$\frac{1}{4}$ teaspoon dried thyme, crumbled
$\frac{1}{4}$ teaspoon dried oregano, crumbled

$\frac{1}{4}$ teaspoon dried basil, crumbled
12 tablespoons (1$\frac{1}{2}$ sticks) butter, melted
8 boneless, skinless fish fillets (about $\frac{1}{4}$ pound each)
Lemon wedges

On a deep plate, combine all the seasonings and mix till well blended. Pour the butter into a bowl. Dip the fish fillets in the butter, sprinkle the seasoned mixture on both sides, and place on a platter.

Heat a large cast-iron skillet over high heat for about 8 minutes or till smoking hot. Add half of the fish fillets, drizzle about 1 teaspoon of the butter over each, and fry for about 1$\frac{1}{2}$ minutes. (The butter may flame up, so be careful.) Turn the fish, drizzle each fillet with another teaspoon of butter, fry for 1$\frac{1}{2}$ minutes longer, and transfer to a clean platter. Repeat the procedure with the remaining fillets, then serve immediately with lemon wedges.

Catawba Pecan-Crusted Catfish

MAKES 6 SERVINGS

Fried catfish has been a staple of Southern cooking for centuries, and for me no memory is sharper than the catfish fries I attended as a youngster on the banks of the Catawba River outside Charlotte, North Carolina. (The Southern commercial catfish industry is now enormous, and in Mississippi alone there are no less than 100,000 acres of catfish farms.) While sweet catfish can be baked, broiled, poached, and served with various sauces, all Southerners agree there is generally nothing to equal shallow- or deep-fried catfish with a simple tartar sauce, and for something really special and packed with Dixie flavor, fried catfish with a crunchy cornmeal-pecan crust is a dish worthy of the most sophisticated table. What to serve with fried catfish? Bowls of coleslaw and baskets of hush puppies, of course—and ketchup!

½ cup yellow cornmeal
½ cup finely chopped pecans
Salt and freshly ground black pepper to taste

Tabasco sauce to taste
6 catfish fillets (about 6 ounces each)
6 tablespoons peanut oil

On a large plate, combine the cornmeal, pecans, salt and pepper, and Tabasco and mix till well blended. Dredge the catfish in the mixture to coat well and place on another large plate.

In a large cast-iron skillet, heat 3 tablespoons of the oil over moderately high heat, add 3 of the fillets, and fry till golden brown, about 4 minutes on each side. Drain briefly on paper towels, place on a heated serving platter, and cover with foil to keep hot while frying the remaining 3 fillets in the remaining 3 tablespoons oil. Serve immediately.

Herbed Catfish Fingers

MAKES 4 SERVINGS

Although sweet catfish is prepared every way imaginable throughout the South, most Rebs agree that no fish lends itself more to deep frying—and the simpler the procedure, the better. Since, however, catfish can be rather bland, a few herbs added to a tangy buttermilk batter can do wonders to enhance the overall flavor. These clever fingers should be fried just till they're crunchy on the outside but still moist inside, and so long as you maintain the temperature of the oil at 365°F, they should not be at all greasy. Any style of zesty cocktail sauce can be served with the fish, but real fried catfish lovers opt for one accompaniment and one only: lots of plain ketchup.

---

4 fresh catfish fillets (about 6 ounces each)
½ cup buttermilk
1 garlic clove, minced
½ teaspoon dried thyme, crumbled
½ teaspoon dried rosemary, crumbled

Salt and freshly ground black pepper to taste
Tabasco sauce to taste
1½ cups all-purpose flour
Vegetable oil for deep frying

Cut the catfish fillets into fingers about 3 inches long and 1 inch wide and place in a bowl. Add the buttermilk, garlic, thyme, rosemary, salt and pepper, and Tabasco, toss, and let stand for about 15 minutes. Place the flour in a brown paper bag.

In a deep fryer, heat about 2 inches of oil to 365°F on a deep-fat thermometer.

Place the catfish fingers in the paper bag and shake to coat evenly. In batches, fry the fingers in the oil till golden brown, about 5 minutes, drain on paper towels, and serve immediately.

Blue Ridge Trout with Bacon-Cream Sauce

MAKES 4 SERVINGS

Some of the best trout fishing in the country is to be found in the rivers of the Great Smoky Mountains of Tennessee and North Carolina, and whether it's a question of a cozy inn or backyard fish fry, locals agree that no cooking method brings out the trout's sweet succulence like simple frying in bacon drippings. Small brook or speckled trout are available fresh in most seafood markets, but since the flesh is firm-textured with a medium fat content, frozen trout is fully acceptable if necessary. In either case, just be careful not to overcook the fish. Perfectly fried trout needs no adornment, but this sauce does transform it into quite an elegant dish.

6 slices lean bacon
1 cup all-purpose flour
Salt and freshly ground black pepper to taste
Cayenne pepper to taste

4 medium fresh trout, dressed
1 cup half-and-half
2 tablespoons minced fresh chives

In a large, heavy skillet, fry the bacon over moderate heat till crisp, drain on paper towels, and crumble, reserving the bacon drippings in the skillet.

On a plate, mix together the flour, salt and pepper, and cayenne and dredge the trout on both sides in the mixture. Fry the trout in the bacon drippings over moderate heat till golden brown, 4 to 5 minutes on each side. Add the half-and-half and chives and simmer till bubbly. Add the crumbled bacon and stir till well blended in the sauce.

To serve, arrange the trout on serving plates and spoon the sauce over the top.

Outer Banks Fish Cakes

MAKES 4 TO 6 SERVINGS

Visit any of the casual seafood shacks around Ocracoke Island on North Carolina's Outer Banks (as well as on some of Georgia's offshore islands), and you're almost sure to find various styles of delectable fried fish cakes made with a combination of lean and fat fish for just the right flavor and texture. When shopping, you might remember that sea bass and salmon make a perfect union for these cakes, but depending on what's available fresh and looks best, you might also combine lean halibut with fatty bluefish or trout with grouper or red snapper. Do note that fish cakes tend to be greasy even when fried over high heat and that nothing is better for draining than brown paper bags.

1½ pounds mixed fish fillets (sea bass, grouper, mackerel, red snapper, bluefish)

1 whole lemon, cut in half

3 black peppercorns

½ bay leaf

3 scallions (part of green tops included), minced

½ cup finely chopped fresh parsley leaves

1 large egg, beaten

3 tablespoons mayonnaise

1 tablespoon fresh lemon juice

2 tablespoons Dijon mustard

1 tablespoon Worcestershire sauce

Tabasco sauce to taste

Salt and freshly ground black pepper to taste

½ cup dry bread crumbs

⅓ cup vegetable oil

Lemon wedges

Arrange the fish fillets in a large nonreactive skillet, add enough water to barely cover them, squeeze the lemon halves into the water, and add the peppercorns and bay leaf. Bring the water to a low simmer, cover, and cook till the fish flakes, about 10 minutes. Transfer the fish to a plate, let cool completely, remove any skin, then flake well with a fork.

Place the flaked fish in a bowl, add all the remaining ingredients except the vegetable oil and lemon wedges, and mix gently till the ingredients just hold together. Form the mixture into 4 to 6 oval cakes and place on a plate.

In a large, heavy skillet, heat the oil over moderately high heat till a morsel of bread tossed in the pan sizzles, add the fish cakes, and fry till golden brown, about 4 minutes on each side. Drain on brown paper bags and serve hot with the lemon wedges.

Sunday Supper Tuna Croquettes

MAKES 4 SERVINGS

While the rest of the country exploits fresh tuna in every guise imaginable, most Southerners (myself included) still relish the ordinary canned product and have come up with numerous ways to use it in cooking. Served with a mess of fried okra and a big basket of fresh cornbread, these crispy croquettes are ideal for a simple Sunday supper and illustrate just how versatile and delicious canned tuna can be when handled with a bit of imagination. So long as you don't burn the croquettes, this is one time you don't have to worry much about overcooking.

Two 5-ounce cans solid white tuna, drained
1 small onion, finely chopped
1 small green bell pepper, seeded and finely chopped
2 large eggs, beaten

3 tablespoons all-purpose flour
1 tablespoon Worcestershire sauce
Salt and freshly ground black pepper to taste
Cayenne pepper to taste
¼ cup vegetable oil

In a bowl, combine the tuna, onion, bell pepper, eggs, flour, Worcestershire, salt and pepper, and cayenne and mix till well blended and smooth. Form the mixture into 4 croquettes and place on a plate.

In a large, heavy skillet, heat the oil over moderately high heat, add the croquettes, and fry till golden brown, about 3 minutes on each side, turning once. Drain on paper towels and serve hot.

Dilled Fresh Salmon Cakes

MAKES 4 SERVINGS

There's nothing wrong with using top-grade pink or red canned salmon for these buttery cakes, but why go to that expense when leftover poached or grilled salmon steaks are so much better and certainly easier on the budget? Likewise, this is one time when fresh dill makes all the difference in the world, so shop accordingly. Serve the cakes with French fries, coleslaw, and maybe some fried dill pickles, and while some Southerners like tartar sauce with any style of fish cake, I personally prefer only a good squeeze of lemon on mine.

---

2 cups finely flaked poached or grilled salmon
Juice of 1 lemon
1 teaspoon dry mustard
¼ cup chopped fresh parsley leaves
1 tablespoon chopped fresh chives
1 tablespoon minced fresh dill
1 tablespoon finely chopped drained capers

½ cup mayonnaise
1 to 1½ cups fresh bread crumbs
¼ cup chicken broth
Paprika to taste
Fine dry bread crumbs, for dredging
6 tablespoons (¾ stick) butter
Fresh lemon wedges

In a large bowl, combine the salmon, lemon juice, dry mustard, parsley, chives, dill, capers, and mayonnaise and toss till well blended. Add enough of the fresh bread crumbs to tighten the mixture, then add enough chicken broth to produce a firm but moist consistency.

Using your hands, form the mixture into 4 oval cakes and brush both sides with a little chicken broth. Sprinkle each with paprika and roll lightly in the dry bread crumbs.

In a large, heavy skillet, melt the butter over moderate heat, add the cakes, and fry till golden brown, 4 to 5 minutes on each side. Drain on paper towels and serve warm with lemon wedges.

Spicy Chesapeake Bay Oyster Pan Roast

MAKES 4 SERVINGS

In coastal Virginia, the Carolinas, and Georgia, a traditional oyster roast is a festive outdoor event involving pounds of oysters in the shell cooked on large gridirons over live coals and eaten with only melted butter. In Maryland's Chesapeake Bay area, however, nothing is relished more than shelled bluepoints, Chincoteagues, and other local varieties that are simply fried ("pan roasted") and served with a special hot cocktail sauce. Typically, the oysters are not battered, but they are always served on slices of buttered toast, and oyster eating just doesn't come any better. Take care not to overcook these oysters—cook only till they begin to plump and curl.

---

4 tablespoons (½ stick) butter
1 pint shucked fresh oysters, drained and
   patted dry
4 slices toast, buttered
2 tablespoons ketchup

1 teaspoon fresh lemon juice
1 teaspoon Worcestershire sauce
Salt and freshly ground black pepper to taste
Tabasco sauce to taste

In a large, heavy skillet, melt the butter over moderate heat, add the oysters, and fry just till they plump and begin to curl, 3 to 4 minutes, turning once. Arrange the toast on serving plates and spoon equal amounts of the oysters over the tops.

Add the ketchup, lemon juice, Worcestershire, salt and pepper, and Tabasco to the skillet, stir for about 1 minute, spoon the sauce over the oysters, and serve hot.

Gulf Coast Oyster and Corn Fritters

MAKES 4 TO 6 SERVINGS

Not till I was first served these succulent fritters at a family cookout on Florida's Gulf Coast did I become aware of the amazing affinity of oysters and corn. It helped, of course, that the oysters were the superior fat Gulf bivalves found all along the Florida and Louisiana coasts, and that the corn had been scraped from cobs right from the field, but this doesn't mean you can't make delicious fritters using whatever fresh oysters are available and, if necessary, frozen corn. Served with ham biscuits or buttered cornbread, the fritters are both unusual and memorable.

1 cup chopped fresh oysters
1 cup corn kernels (fresh or thawed frozen)
2 large eggs, beaten
6 tablespoons all-purpose flour
Salt and freshly ground black pepper to taste

Cayenne pepper to taste
⅓ cup milk
¼ cup corn oil
2 tablespoons butter

In a large bowl, combine the oysters, corn, and eggs and toss till well blended. Add the flour, salt and pepper, and cayenne and stir till well blended. Add the milk and stir till the batter is well blended and smooth.

In a large, heavy skillet, heat 2 tablespoons of the oil and 1 tablespoon of the butter over moderately high heat, spoon about 4 mounds of the batter into the fat, or just enough at a time to fill the skillet, and fry till golden brown on both sides, about 8 minutes in all, turning once. Drain the fritters on paper towels, repeat with the remaining oil, butter, and batter, and keep the fritters hot till ready to serve.

Frank's Fried Oysters with Remoulade Sauce

MAKES 4 SERVINGS

When it comes to the Southern art of frying oysters, nobody has mastered the technique better than owner-chef Frank Stitt at Highlands Bar & Grill in Birmingham, Alabama. When he serves his beauties in oyster shells with this sumptuous remoulade sauce, the memory won't fade anytime soon. For the right texture, be sure to maintain the temperature of the oil while frying the oysters in batches, and never cook them for more than a couple of minutes—or just till barely browned.

1 cup mayonnaise
2 tablespoons minced dill pickles
2 tablespoons minced fresh parsley leaves
2 tablespoons minced drained capers
1 tablespoon minced scallions
1 tablespoon minced drained anchovies
1 tablespoon whole-grain mustard
1 tablespoon minced fresh tarragon leaves
2 tablespoons sherry vinegar
½ teaspoon paprika

½ teaspoon fresh lemon juice
Salt and freshly ground black pepper to taste
Tabasco sauce to taste
2 cups cornmeal
1 cup all-purpose flour
Peanut oil for deep frying
24 fresh oysters, shucked and bottom shells reserved
2 cups buttermilk

In a bowl, combine the mayonnaise, pickles, parsley, capers, scallions, anchovies, mustard, tarragon, vinegar, paprika, lemon juice, salt and pepper, and Tabasco, stir till well blended, cover with plastic wrap, and set the remoulade sauce aside.

In a shallow dish, combine the cornmeal, flour, and salt and pepper to taste and mix till well blended.

In a deep fryer or cast-iron pot, heat about 2 inches of oil to 365°F on a deep-fat thermometer.

In batches, dip the oysters in buttermilk, then in the cornmeal mixture, tossing to coat, and fry till golden brown and crisp, about 2 minutes. Using a slotted spoon, transfer the oysters to paper towels to drain.

Spoon a little of the remoulade sauce into each reserved shell and top each with a fried oyster. Serve warm.

New Orleans Oyster Po'boys

MAKES 4 SERVINGS

In New Orleans, the hefty sandwich known as the po'boy can be made with anything from assorted deli meats and cheeses to grilled chicken to fried fish, but by far the most popular and beloved po'boys involve fried local oysters enhanced by shredded lettuce and dill pickle chips—all packed into crispy short loaves of New Orleans French bread spread with mayonnaise. It's a unique sandwich, and even if you can't use genuine New Orleans bread, any baguette-style works almost as well.

---

2 cups yellow cornmeal
1 tablespoon garlic powder
1 tablespoon onion powder
1 tablespoon paprika
1 tablespoon salt
1 tablespoon freshly ground black pepper
1 teaspoon dried thyme, crumbled
1 teaspoon dried oregano, crumbled

½ teaspoon cayenne pepper
35 to 40 fresh oysters, shucked and drained
Peanut oil for deep frying
Four 8-inch-long French baguettes, split
Mayonnaise
Shredded iceberg lettuce
Dill pickle chips

In a bowl, combine the cornmeal, garlic powder, onion powder, paprika, salt, black pepper, thyme, oregano, and cayenne and stir till well blended. Add the oysters, toss to coat well, and place on a platter.

In a Dutch oven or large saucepan, heat about 2 inches of oil to 365°F on a deep-fat thermometer, fry the oysters in batches till golden brown, 2 to 3 minutes, and drain on paper towels.

Spread the insides of each baguette with mayonnaise, divide the oysters on one half of each, sprinkle lettuce and pickles over the oysters, and top with the other halves of bread. Eat with the hands.

Classy Butter-Fried Oysters

MAKES 4 TO 6 SERVINGS

If you like your oysters unadorned, rich, and mellow, nothing equals battering them as simply as possible, then shallow-frying them to a crispy finish in plenty of butter. You can always serve these elegant fried oysters with a spicy cocktail sauce, but purists opt for nothing but fresh lemon juice squeezed over the tops. To prevent burning the oysters, be sure to add a couple of tablespoons of cooking oil to the hot butter (or use only clarified butter), and never crowd the oysters in the pan, always frying them in batches and using a slotted spoon to lift them in and out of the fat.

1 cup all-purpose flour
Salt and freshly ground black pepper to taste
4 cups bread crumbs
24 fresh oysters, shucked and drained

2 large eggs, beaten
1 pound (4 sticks) butter
2 tablespoons vegetable oil
Lemon wedges

In a bowl, combine the flour and salt and pepper, and mix till well blended. Spread the bread crumbs on a baking sheet.

Dip each oyster in the seasoned flour, then in the egg, and coat well with the bread crumbs.

In a large, heavy cast-iron skillet, melt the butter over moderately high heat and add the oil. When a few bread crumbs tossed into the fat sputter and brown quickly, fry the oysters in batches till golden and crisp, about 2 minutes, turning once, and drain on paper towels. Serve the oysters with lemon wedges.

Spiced Skillet Shrimp

MAKES 4 SERVINGS

Fried shrimp is a staple all over the South, and cooks are always coming up with new and unusual ways to enhance the dish. Here, virtually any spices can be used to infuse flavor into the cooking oil, so long, that is, as you don't overwhelm the delectable flavor of the shrimp. Remember also that frying the shrimp for more than a couple of minutes will only toughen them.

¼ cup peanut oil
1 tablespoon shredded peeled fresh ginger
1 teaspoon whole allspice berries
1 teaspoon whole fennel seeds

1 pound fresh large shrimp, shelled and
  deveined but tails left intact
Salt and freshly ground black pepper to taste
½ lemon
2 tablespoons minced fresh chives

In a large, heavy skillet, heat the oil over moderately high heat for about 2 minutes, add the ginger, allspice berries, and fennel seeds, and stir till the ginger turns light brown, about 2 minutes. Add the shrimp and, using a slotted spoon, fry them till they turn pink and curl, about 2 minutes, tossing. Lift the shrimp out with the spoon and transfer to a serving platter, season with salt and pepper, squeeze the lemon over the top, and sprinkle with the chives. Serve hot.

Buttermilk-Battered Fried Shrimp

MAKES 6 SERVINGS

No seafood is more relished and popular throughout the South than fried shrimp, and savvy cooks know that one of the best ways to make the crispy shrimp satiny and succulent on the inside is to dip them into buttermilk batter before dredging in cracker crumbs and deep-frying them fairly quickly. It's also common knowledge that, especially when draining fried shrimp, nothing absorbs grease better than brown paper bags. Depending on the social occasion, you might want to leave the tails of the shrimp intact while cleaning them to help those who prefer to eat with the fingers, and it's always a good idea to have a bowl of cocktail sauce on the side whenever any fried shrimp is served.

1½ cups crushed soda crackers
½ cup all-purpose flour
Salt and freshly ground black pepper to taste
½ cup buttermilk
1 large egg

Tabasco sauce to taste
2 pounds fresh large shrimp, shelled and
  deveined
Vegetable oil for deep frying

In a shallow dish, combine the crackers, flour, and salt and pepper and mix till well blended. In a bowl, combine the buttermilk, egg, and Tabasco and beat till well blended.

Dip the shrimp into the buttermilk mixture, dredge in the cracker mixture, and place on a platter.

In a large, deep cast-iron skillet, heat about 2 inches of oil to 365°F on a deep–fat thermometer, fry the shrimp in batches till golden, about 2 minutes, and drain on brown paper bags or paper towels. Serve hot.

Clam Fritters with Tartar Sauce

MAKES 6 SERVINGS

Although fresh hard-shell quahogs are plentiful and raked all along the coastal Southern states, I usually prefer to cook with canned baby clams since they are not only tender and fully acceptable in flavor but pose much less risk of overcooking (and toughening). Still, be sure to watch these fritters carefully and remove them from the oil as soon as they're just fried through and lightly browned. Some cooks dredge their batter in plain flour, but I find that cornmeal provides a much tastier and more delightful crunch to the fritters. This is a classic tartar sauce suitable for virtually any form of fried seafood, so you may want to double the recipe and have plenty of sauce on hand in the fridge.

THE TARTAR SAUCE
1 cup mayonnaise
1 tablespoon drained sweet pickle relish
1 tablespoon minced fresh parsley leaves
1 tablespoon minced scallions
2 teaspoons minced drained capers
1 teaspoon Dijon mustard

THE FRITTERS
Two 10½-ounce cans minced clams, drained and juice reserved

2 large eggs, beaten
1 teaspoon fresh lemon juice
1 tablespoon finely chopped fresh parsley leaves
2 cups yellow cornmeal
2 teaspoons baking soda
½ cup milk
3 tablespoons butter, melted
Salt and freshly ground black pepper to taste
Cayenne pepper to taste
Peanut oil for deep frying

 To keep fats as clean as possible and reduce discoloration and off flavors in foods, remove crumbs, morsels of batter, and other such particles with a slotted spoon or spider as you fry.

To make the sauce, combine all the ingredients in a bowl, mix till well blended, and let stand at room temperature for 15 minutes. Chill till ready to serve.

To make the fritters, combine the clams, eggs, lemon juice, parsley, cornmeal, and baking soda in a large bowl and stir till well blended. Blend the reserved clam juice with the milk and add just enough to the clam mixture to make a firm batter, stirring well. Add the butter, salt and pepper, and cayenne and stir till well blended.

In a large, heavy skillet, heat about 1 inch of oil over moderate heat for 2 minutes, drop the batter by full tablespoons in batches into the oil, and fry till cooked through and browned, 2 to 3 minutes, turning once. Drain the fritters on paper towels and serve hot with the tartar sauce.

Popcorn Crawfish

MAKES 4 SERVINGS

I must have half a dozen different recipes for this extraordinary dish, popularized in New Orleans by the legendary Cajun chef Paul Prudhomme back in the 1980s, but this one is the simplest and easiest, and since it is not overwhelmed by multiple seasonings, it makes an ideal main course, served with perhaps a hearty Cajun maque choux (see page 184) and various pickles and relishes. Accompanied by a tartar or remoulade sauce for dipping, crispy popcorn crawfish (or "Cajun popcorn") is also sensational finger food at cocktail and wedding receptions—and the spicier the better. If you have trouble finding frozen crawfish tails, medium shelled and deveined fresh shrimp can be substituted. Popcorn crawfish must be served immediately after frying, for when it is allowed to cool, it becomes dreadfully soggy and unappetizing.

---

1 pound shelled crawfish tails (fresh or
   thawed frozen)
½ cup milk whisked with 1 large egg
½ teaspoon dried thyme, crumbled

1 teaspoon salt
¼ teaspoon Tabasco sauce
1½ cups dry bread crumbs
Peanut oil for deep frying

In a bowl, combine the crawfish tails, milk-egg mixture, thyme, salt, and Tabasco, toss well, and let stand for about 15 minutes. Place the bread crumbs in a brown paper bag.

In a deep fryer, electric frypan, or large cast-iron skillet, heat about 1½ inches of oil to 365°F on a deep-fat thermometer.

Place the crawfish in the paper bag, shake to coat evenly with the bread crumbs, fry in batches till golden, about 3 minutes, never allowing the temperature of the oil to fall below 365°F, and drain on paper towels. Serve immediately.

Carolina Pan-Fried Soft-Shell Crabs

MAKES 6 SERVINGS

Considered a great delicacy all along the Atlantic and Gulf coasts in the South, soft-shell crabs are mostly blue crabs that have molted their hard shells to grow larger ones, and they are always either sautéed whole in butter or shallow-fried in oil to a crispy finish. I've eaten soft-shells from Maryland to Louisiana, and while there's certainly nothing wrong with crabs that are simply fried and served with only a few squeezes of lemon, without question some of the most memorable were those that master chef Louis Osteen soaked in buttermilk, fried, and enhanced with a luscious butter-vinegar sauce at his restaurant on Pawleys Island, South Carolina.

---

6 soft-shell crabs, rinsed
Buttermilk
1 cup all-purpose flour
1 cup yellow cornmeal
½ teaspoon baking soda

Salt and freshly ground black pepper to taste
Peanut oil for shallow frying
2 tablespoons fresh lemon juice
1 tablespoon red wine vinegar
12 tablespoons (1½ sticks) butter, cut into pieces

Place the crabs in a baking dish, add enough buttermilk to barely cover, and let stand for about 30 minutes.

On a plate, combine the flour, cornmeal, baking soda, and salt and pepper and mix till well blended. Remove the crabs from the buttermilk, dredge all over in the dry mixture, and place on another plate.

In a large cast-iron skillet, heat about 1 inch of oil to 365°F on a deep-fat thermometer, fry half the crabs till golden brown, about 2 minutes on each side, turning once, and drain on paper towels. Repeat with the remaining crabs.

Pour off the oil from the skillet, add the lemon juice and vinegar, and stir over moderate heat, scraping up browned bits from the bottom of the pan. Add the butter in pieces, whisking till the sauce is thickened and smooth.

To serve, place the crabs on serving plates and spoon the butter sauce over the top.

Classic Maryland Crab Cakes

MAKES 4 SERVINGS

Don't ask me why Marylanders have a special way with crab cakes, but I suspect it has lots to do with handling them as little as possible (the less you mix the crabmeat, the lighter the cakes), using minimum breading, and frying the cakes briefly in nothing but butter. Whatever the secret, I've eaten the specialty from Baltimore to Grasonville to Annapolis, studied the various formulas and techniques, and concluded, all modesty aside, that this is the one and only way to produce a genuine Maryland crab cake. You can serve the cakes with a tartar or mustard sauce, but in the final analysis, all they really need is a few squeezes of fresh lemon juice.

---

1 cup mayonnaise
1 large egg white
1 tablespoon fresh lemon juice
1 tablespoon minced scallions
3 tablespoons finely crushed soda crackers
$\frac{1}{8}$ teaspoon cayenne pepper

1½ pounds fresh lump crabmeat, picked over
   for shells and cartilage
¾ cup fine, dry bread crumbs
4 tablespoons (½ stick) butter
Lemon wedges

In a bowl, combine the mayonnaise, egg white, lemon juice, scallions, cracker crumbs, and cayenne and mix till well blended. Add the crabmeat and toss very gently but thoroughly. Divide the mixture into 4 equal portions and gently shape each into a patty. Spread the bread crumbs on a baking sheet and coat the patties lightly but firmly. Chill the patties, covered, for at least 1 hour.

In a large, heavy skillet, melt the butter over moderate heat for 2 minutes, add the crab cakes, and fry till golden brown, about 3 minutes on each side. Serve immediately with lemon wedges.

Vegetables

Carolina Okra Beignets

MAKES 4 SERVINGS

These spicy beignets were inspired by the ones Bill Neal fried up when he opened Crook's Corner restaurant in Chapel Hill, North Carolina, and, quite frankly, you'll never taste a more delicious okra dish. Just remember never to crowd the skillet when frying the beignets, and don't try to keep them warm in the oven, which only makes them soggy. When shopping for fresh okra, always look for small, firm pods with no dark spots.

1 pound small, firm, fresh okra
2 medium onions, minced
½ small green bell pepper, seeded and
  minced
3 tablespoons all-purpose flour
¼ cup fine dry bread crumbs

½ teaspoon salt, plus more as needed
1 large egg
1 tablespoon half-and-half
½ teaspoon Tabasco sauce
Vegetable shortening for deep frying

Rinse the okra, remove the stems, and thinly slice the pods. In a bowl, combine the okra, onions, and bell pepper and toss till well blended. Add the flour, bread crumbs, and ½ teaspoon salt and toss again. In a small bowl, whisk together the egg, half-and-half, and Tabasco till well blended, pour over the okra mixture, stir till well blended, and let stand for about 30 minutes.

In a large, heavy skillet, heat about 1 inch of shortening to 375°F on a deep-fat thermometer, drop the okra mixture by tablespoons into the hot fat, fry till golden brown and crisp on all sides, 3 to 4 minutes, and transfer with a slotted spoon to paper towels to drain. If you like, sprinkle with a little extra salt. Serve piping hot.

Classic Batter-Fried Okra

MAKES 4 SERVINGS

No vegetable is more loved and respected in the South than okra, and even Yankees repelled by just the sight of slimy boiled pods become addicted to fried okra after the first bite. The real trick to crisp fried okra is soaking it in ice water before frying it in lard, and remember never to crowd the fryer or skillet if you want even browning. Only fresh okra (preferably small, firm pods with no dark spots) should be fried, and to prevent sogginess, fried okra should never be kept warm in the oven. Serve the okra rounds as a side dish or with cocktails.

1½ pounds small, firm, fresh okra	1 cup regular buttermilk
1 cup white cornmeal or fine cracker crumbs	1 large egg, beaten
1 teaspoon salt, plus more as needed	Tabasco sauce to taste
Freshly ground black pepper to taste	Lard for deep frying

Rinse the okra, remove the stems, and cut the pods into ½-inch rounds. Place in a large bowl with enough ice water to cover and let soak for 15 minutes. Drain the okra, pat dry with paper towels, and set aside.

In a shallow bowl, combine the cornmeal, 1 teaspoon salt, pepper, buttermilk, egg, and Tabasco and beat till the batter is smooth.

In a deep fryer or large cast-iron skillet, heat about ½ inch of lard to 375°F on a deep-fat thermometer. In batches, dip the okra in the batter till well coated, carefully drop it into the fat without overcrowding, and fry till golden brown and crisp, 3 to 4 minutes. With a slotted spoon, transfer the okra to a large baking sheet covered with paper towels to drain, sprinkle with a little extra salt, and serve hot.

Texas Corn Fritters

MAKES 4 TO 6 SERVINGS

These are the small, light, fluffy corn fritters that an old friend always served with baked country ham at her home in Houston and that I now fry up to accompany virtually any pork dish. Since the flavorful liquid in canned corn is essential for this batter, do not try to substitute fresh or frozen corn for these particular fritters. For enhanced flavor, you might also add a pinch or so of dried herbs to the dry mixture before blending in the milk mixture and corn.

One 16- to 17-ounce can whole corn kernels
   with juice
$\frac{1}{3}$ cup evaporated milk
2 large eggs

$1\frac{1}{2}$ cups all-purpose flour
2 teaspoons baking powder
Salt and freshly ground black pepper to taste
Corn oil for shallow frying

Drain the corn, reserving the liquid. In a bowl, combine the corn liquid and milk to measure $\frac{1}{2}$ cup, add the eggs, and whisk till well blended. In another bowl, combine the flour, baking powder, and salt and pepper, stir, add the milk mixture, and stir till well blended and smooth. Stir in the corn kernels.

In a large, heavy skillet, heat about 1 inch of oil to 365°F on a deep-fat thermometer. In batches, drop the corn mixture into the oil by heaping tablespoons, not crowding the pan, and fry till golden brown, about 4 minutes, turning once. Drain on paper towels and serve as hot as possible.

Kentucky Fried Corn

MAKES 4 SERVINGS

Served at breakfast and with virtually any pork dish, fried corn has to be one of the most distinctive and delicious of all Southern vegetable preparations and one you're not likely to find anywhere outside the region. While frozen (but not canned) corn can be fried successfully in this manner, nothing equals kernels (with their milk) cut and scraped from fresh ears, and during the summer months, I always freeze enough fresh corn in individual plastic bags to last well into the winter months. If you like a spicy edge to your corn, by all means add a few sprinklings of cayenne pepper along with the butter.

6 or 7 ears fresh corn, husks and silks removed
3 tablespoons minced onion
3 tablespoons minced green bell pepper
1 tablespoon all-purpose flour

1 tablespoon sugar
Salt and freshly ground black pepper to taste
1 cup whole milk
3 tablespoons bacon grease
2 tablespoons butter

With a sharp knife, cut the corn kernels off the cobs into a bowl (also scraping off the milk), add the onion, bell pepper, flour, sugar, salt and pepper, and milk, and stir till well blended.

In a large cast-iron skillet, heat the bacon grease over moderate heat, add the corn mixture, and fry till part of the liquid has evaporated, about 5 minutes. Add the butter and continue to stir till the butter is melted and the corn is tender, about 10 minutes. Serve hot.

Squash Puppies

MAKES 4 TO 6 SERVINGS

Yellow crookneck squash is now available in most markets not only during the summer months but all year long, and while it is used to make sumptuous soufflés, puddings, and casseroles, never is it more appreciated than when it is blended with onion, garlic, eggs, and Parmesan cheese and fried in the same manner as hush puppies. Just remember that all summer squash is relatively moist and delicate compared with acorn, buttercup, Hubbard, and other winter varieties and dries out quickly if overcooked. These puppies can also be made with raw grated zucchini, winter squash, parsnips, rutabagas, and even sweet potatoes, in which case the frying time is a bit longer for a golden brown finish.

---

4 medium yellow squash, grated
1 small onion, grated
1 garlic clove, minced
6 tablespoons all-purpose flour
¼ cup grated Parmesan cheese

Salt and freshly ground black pepper to taste
2 large eggs, beaten
2 tablespoons butter, melted
Vegetable oil for deep frying

In a bowl, combine all the ingredients except the oil and mix till thoroughly blended and smooth.

In a large, heavy skillet, heat about 1 inch of oil to 365°F on a deep-fat thermometer, drop the squash mixture by tablespoons in batches into the oil, and fry till lightly browned, 3 to 4 minutes, turning once. Drain on paper towels and serve hot or warm.

 The larger the surface area of fried food compared to its volume, the more fat is absorbed, which is why potato chips tend to be greasy.

Country Club Fried Oregano Eggplant

MAKES 4 OR 5 SERVINGS

Since young, slim eggplants don't need to be peeled or salted and leached of excess moisture, these are the ones Southern cooks go out of their way to find when they want to fry elegant rounds of eggplant like those that grace so many country club buffet tables. If you must use a large (and often bitter) eggplant, peel it, cut it into ½-inch-thick rounds, salt the rounds, and let drain on paper towels for about 30 minutes before frying. Eggplant fries very quickly, so be sure to remove it from the oil the second it begins to brown. If you like, a little grated Parmesan cheese sprinkled over the hot rounds is always a nice option.

---

2 large eggs, beaten
½ teaspoon dried oregano, crumbled
⅛ teaspoon grated nutmeg
Freshly ground black pepper to taste

6 small eggplants (not peeled), cut into
  ½-inch-thick rounds
½ cup cracker crumbs
½ cup peanut oil

In a bowl, combine the eggs, oregano, nutmeg, and pepper and stir till well blended. Dip the eggplant rounds into the egg mixture, then in the cracker crumbs, and place on a plate.

In a large, heavy skillet, heat 3 to 4 tablespoons of the oil for about 2 minutes over moderately high heat, add the eggplant rounds in batches, adding more oil as needed, fry till browned, about 1 minute on each side, and drain on paper towels. Serve immediately.

Fried Rosemary Zucchini

MAKES 4 TO 6 SERVINGS

Deep-fried zucchini rounds are relished as much on the Southern table as anywhere else, but savvy cooks know that if the rounds are to fry up nicely browned and crispy, they must first be salted and drained of excess water. When shopping, look for zucchini about 6 inches long and 2 inches thick with skins that are free of blemishes and have a vibrant green color. Be sure to taste the fried rounds before possibly salting them; if you like, they can also be sprinkled lightly with grated Parmesan cheese.

3 medium zucchini, trimmed and sliced into
   ½-inch-thick rounds
Salt to taste
1 cup all-purpose flour
2 large eggs
1 garlic clove, minced

1 teaspoon minced fresh rosemary leaves
Freshly ground black pepper to taste
1 cup dry bread crumbs
Vegetable oil for deep frying
Lemon wedges

Place the zucchini rounds in a large colander in the sink, sprinkle lightly with salt, tossing, and let stand for 20 minutes to drain. Pat the rounds dry with paper towels and set aside.

Place the flour in a bowl. In another bowl, whisk together the eggs, garlic, rosemary, and pepper till well blended. In a third bowl, place the bread crumbs.

In a deep fryer or heavy saucepan, heat about 1 inch of oil to 365°F on a deep-fat thermometer and fry the zucchini in batches till golden brown and crisp, about 2 minutes, turning once with a slotted spoon. Drain on paper towels, season with extra salt, and serve hot or warm with lemon wedges.

Stir-Fried Broccoli with Garlic and Parmesan

MAKES 4 SERVINGS

If you prefer fresh broccoli almost raw (most Southerners don't), you may want to dispense with the pre-steaming altogether and simply stir-fry the pieces till they're just crisp-tender. Nor is the cheese necessary if you truly love the full flavor of broccoli, in which case an extra tablespoon of olive oil might be used.

One 2-pound head broccoli	Salt and freshly ground black pepper to taste
3 tablespoons olive oil	½ lemon
1 garlic clove, minced	½ cup grated Parmesan cheese

Remove and discard any coarse stem ends and leaves of the broccoli and separate the stalks. Place the stalks in a large, heavy skillet with enough water to cover, bring to a simmer, cover, let steam till softened, 7 to 8 minutes, and drain. Cut the broccoli into 2-inch lengths.

Dry the skillet, then heat the olive oil over moderate heat, add the garlic, and stir for 1 minute. Add the broccoli and salt and pepper, stir-fry for 3 minutes, squeeze the lemon over the top, and stir-fry for about 2 minutes longer. Add the cheese, stir, cover, cook for about 1 minute longer, and serve hot.

Stir-Fried Collard Greens with Hot Bacon-Vinegar Dressing

MAKES 4 SERVINGS

Boiled collard greens can be bitter and tough, reason enough for some Southern cooks to stir-fry them with bacon (or salt pork) till crisp-tender and fully succulent. Turnip greens, spinach, dandelion greens, and cabbage can be stir-fried in the same manner with equally tasty results. Do try to find small, young collards with tender leaves. I always serve any collards with a cruet of hot pepper vinegar to be drizzled over the top.

---

1 pound young collard greens
4 thick slices lean bacon, cut into small pieces
1 small red onion, chopped

1 garlic clove, minced
2 tablespoons cider vinegar
1 tablespoon dark brown sugar
Salt and freshly ground black pepper to taste

Rinse the collards well, remove and discard any tough stems and discolored leaves, tear the green leaves into small pieces, and place in a bowl.

In a large, heavy skillet, fry the bacon over moderate heat till almost crisp and carefully pour off all but about 2 tablespoons of the drippings. Add the onion and garlic and stir till softened, about 2 minutes. Add the vinegar and sugar to the skillet and stir well till the sugar dissolves. Add the collards, season with salt and pepper, and stir till the collards begin to wilt. Cover the pan, reduce the heat to low, and cook till the collards are crisp-tender, about 10 minutes, stirring occasionally. Serve hot or warm.

Cauliflower Fries

MAKES 6 SERVINGS

Cauliflower is generally boiled, steamed, or baked in kitchens all over the country, but Southern cooks learned long ago that when the florets are briefly parboiled, then generously coated with a cheesy batter and shallow-fried, the vegetable takes on a whole new identity that is utterly beguiling. Fried cauliflower, however, can burn quickly if not watched constantly, which is one reason I use a highly polyunsaturated oil such as safflower, with its ideal smoke point. Serve this cauliflower with any roasted meats or poultry—or even with beef steaks or burgers.

1 large head cauliflower, cored and cut into
  bite-size florets
Salt to taste
2 cups all-purpose flour
1½ cups grated Parmesan cheese

Freshly ground black pepper to taste
2 large eggs, beaten
2 cups milk
Safflower oil for shallow frying

Place the cauliflower florets in a large pot with enough salted water to cover, bring to a boil, reduce the heat to moderate, and cook till the florets are crisp-tender, about 5 minutes. Drain in a colander and set aside.

In a bowl, combine the flour, ½ cup of the cheese, pepper, eggs, and milk and stir to make a smooth batter.

In a large, heavy skillet, heat about 1 inch of oil over moderately high heat for 2 minutes. In batches, dip the florets in the batter to coat thickly and, using a slotted spoon, fry them till golden brown all over, 5 to 6 minutes, turning. Drain on paper towels, sprinkle the florets generously with the remaining 1 cup cheese, and serve hot or at room temperature.

Tennessee Fried Cabbage with Bacon

MAKES 4 TO 6 SERVINGS

Cabbage is as much a Southern staple as field peas, corn, and sweet potatoes, and while cooks in some states elevate the humble vegetable in various casseroles, puddings, and "scallops," those in the mountains of Tennessee pride themselves on nothing more than local cabbage that is simply shredded, fried with bacon, salt pork, or country ham and a little vinegar, and served with fried pork chops, rabbit, pigs' ears, and the like. If you like your cabbage crisp-tender (most Southerners don't), simmer it for no longer than about 20 minutes.

---

1 medium head green cabbage
4 slices bacon, coarsely chopped
1 medium onion, coarsely chopped
1 celery rib, coarsely chopped
2 garlic cloves, minced

3 tablespoons cider vinegar mixed with 1 teaspoon sugar
Salt and freshly ground black pepper to taste
Cayenne pepper to taste

Remove and discard the outer leaves of the cabbage, cut the head in half and remove the core, and shred the halves coarsely.

In a deep, heavy pot, fry the bacon over moderate heat till almost cooked, add the onion, celery, and garlic, and stir till the vegetables are softened, about 3 minutes. Add the vinegar mixture, salt and pepper, and cayenne and stir for 1 minute longer. Add the cabbage and fry, stirring, for about 5 minutes. Cover the pot, reduce the heat to low, and cook till the cabbage is very tender, about 30 minutes, stirring from time to time. Serve hot.

Deep-Fried Wild Mushrooms

MAKES 4 TO 6 SERVINGS

Once was the time when only ordinary commercial button mushrooms were available in Southern markets, but today it's nothing unusual to find fresh shiitakes, morels, chanterelles, ceps, and other fleshy, earthy, pungent wild varieties, all of which are sumptuous when deep fried so long as they're not overcooked. Low in saturated fat and with a rather bland flavor, canola oil is ideal for frying these mushrooms without affecting their distinctive savor and fragrance, and to eat them with fried quail, rabbit, or pheasant is a gustatory treat that's not soon forgotten. To prepare the mushrooms for frying, rinse them lightly of any grit, then dry thoroughly with a kitchen towel.

1¼ cups milk
1 cup all-purpose flour
1 large egg, beaten
½ teaspoon dried thyme, crumbled

Salt and freshly ground black pepper to taste
1 pound wild mushrooms (shiitakes, chanterelles, ceps, or morels) thickly sliced
Canola oil for deep frying

In a bowl, combine the milk, flour, egg, thyme, and salt and pepper and whisk till the batter is smooth. Dip the mushrooms into the batter to coat well on all sides and place on a plate.

In a large, heavy pot, heat about 1½ inches of oil to 350°F on a deep-fat thermometer, fry the mushrooms in batches till golden brown, about 3 minutes, turning with a slotted spoon, and drain on paper towels. Season with extra salt and serve hot or at room temperature.

Georgia Fried Vidalia Onion Rings

MAKES 4 TO 6 SERVINGS

Georgia's indigenous Vidalia onions are the sweetest and most delectable on earth, and when the sweet rings are offset with a tangy buttermilk batter and fried to a golden finish throughout the Peach State, they're served not so much as a mere snack or appetizer as they are a highly respected vegetable at serious meals. Succinctly, if you think you've had great fried onion rings, you've tasted nothing till you've sunk teeth into these rich, crunchy wonders. Vidalias are now available all over the country during the spring and summer months, and each is identified with an official sticker.

2 cups all-purpose flour
Salt and freshly ground black pepper to taste
Cayenne pepper to taste
1 cup buttermilk
2 large eggs, beaten

2 tablespoons peanut oil, plus more as needed
2 large Vidalia onions, cut into ½-inch-thick rings
Peanut oil for deep frying

In a bowl, combine the flour, salt and pepper, and cayenne and stir till well blended. Add the buttermilk, eggs, and 2 tablespoons oil and whisk till the batter is smooth, adding a little more oil if necessary to make a loose batter.

Dip the onion rings in the batter to coat well and place on a platter.

In a deep fryer or deep cast-iron skillet, heat about 2 inches of oil to 375°F on a deep-fat thermometer. In batches, fry the battered rings till golden brown and crunchy, about 4 minutes in all, turning with tongs. Drain on paper towels, season with salt, and serve as hot as possible.

Mississippi Fried Dill Pickles

MAKES ABOUT 2 DOZEN PICKLE CHIPS

Created in the late 1960s at a modest café in Tunica, Mississippi, and originally served with a ranch dipping sauce as an appetizer, fried dill pickles are eaten all over the South with fried catfish, shrimp, and chicken and can quickly become an addiction. By no means use bland hamburger chips for this unique specialty, but rather garlicky, full-flavored kosher dill pickles. If, like most Southerners, you prefer a thick crust on your pickles, dip the chips twice, or even three times, in the batter, and if you want a crisp and golden finish, do not crowd the skillet with too many chips at one time.

1 cup buttermilk
1 large egg
1 cup all-purpose flour
1 teaspoon baking powder

½ teaspoon salt
Vegetable oil for deep frying
4 large, crisp dill pickles, cut widthwise into ¾-inch-thick chips

In a bowl, whisk together the buttermilk and egg till well blended. In another bowl, whisk together the flour, baking powder, and salt, add to the buttermilk mixture, and stir till well blended and smooth.

In a cast–iron skillet, heat about 1 inch of oil to 375°F on a deep–fat thermometer. Dip the pickle chips in the batter to coat evenly, fry a few at a time till golden brown, about 3 minutes, drain on paper towels, and serve hot or at room temperature.

Parsley Fluffs

MAKES 4 SERVINGS

When they say that Southerners will fry anything, this includes even fresh parsley leaves that are squeezed into delectable fluffs, battered, deep-fried till crispy, and served with various types of steaks and chops. Do serve the fluffs as hot as possible, and to prevent sogginess, never cover to keep them warm. Note that this same basic batter can also be used for broccoli and cauliflower florets, cubed turnips and carrots, and sliced summer squash, zucchini, and even sweet potatoes.

1 cup all-purpose flour
2 teaspoons baking powder
1 teaspoon salt
1 cup milk

1 large egg, beaten
3 cups packed fresh parsley leaves, finely chopped
Vegetable shortening or oil for deep frying

In a bowl, combine the flour, baking powder, and salt and mix till well blended. Slowly add the milk and beat till smooth. Add the egg and beat till the batter is well blended and smooth.

With your fingers, squeeze and form the parsley into small compact fluffs, dip the fluffs in the prepared batter to coat lightly, and place on a plate.

In a deep fryer or deep cast–iron skillet, heat about 1 inch of shortening or oil to 375°F on a deep–fat thermometer, drop the fluffs in batches into the fat, fry till golden brown and crisp, about 2 minutes, and drain on paper towels. Serve as hot as possible.

 To "purify" cooking oils, deep-fry a handful of fresh parsley in the oil to absorb most of the offensive odors.

Classic Fried Green Tomatoes

MAKES 4 SERVINGS

Southern fried green tomatoes are justifiably legendary, and when they're battered and fried with care, nothing is more delicious with fried eggs and country sausage patties at breakfast or with grilled meats, fried chicken, or panfried soft-shell crabs. Don't over-batter these tomatoes, and while they can be kept warm without losing much of their toothy crispness, do try to serve them as hot as possible for ultimate enjoyment. As for the tablespoon of bacon grease, fried green tomatoes are simply not genuine without the subtle flavor of bacon.

3 medium fresh, firm green tomatoes	¼ cup all-purpose flour
¼ cup whole milk	Salt and freshly ground black pepper to taste
1 large egg	Peanut oil for shallow frying
1 cup yellow cornmeal	1 tablespoon bacon grease

Cut off and discard the stems of the tomatoes, then cut the tomatoes into ¼-inch-thick slices.

In a bowl, whisk together the milk and egg till well blended. In another bowl, combine the cornmeal, flour, and salt and pepper and stir till well blended.

In a large, heavy skillet, heat about ½ inch of oil plus the bacon grease to 350°F on a deep-fat thermometer. In batches, dip the tomato slices in the milk mixture, then in the cornmeal mixture, shaking off any excess, and fry till golden brown and crisp, about 2 minutes on each side, turning once. Drain on paper towels, sprinkle with extra salt, and keep warm till ready to serve.

 To lighten a cornmeal batter, add a little all-purpose flour to the cornmeal.

Julia's Mixed Vegetable Skillet Succotash

MAKES 6 TO 8 SERVINGS

Leave it to my good friend and colleague from Greenville, Mississippi, Julia Reed, to come up with this luscious fried succotash using a full array of fresh summer vegetables and herbs. By itself, the succotash can be served with everything from fried chicken to meat or poultry croquettes to pork barbecue, but add maybe half a pound of fresh boiled shrimp or cubed cooked chicken to the vegetables at the last minute, and you have a sumptuous and unusual main course.

6 slices bacon
1 medium onion, minced
1 jalapeño chile pepper, seeded and minced
3 garlic cloves, minced
3 cups sliced okra (fresh or thawed frozen)
3 medium ripe tomatoes, peeled and diced

6 ears fresh corn, husks and silks removed
 and kernels cut from the cobs
2 teaspoons chopped fresh thyme leaves
Salt and freshly ground black pepper to taste
Cayenne pepper to taste
8 fresh basil leaves, torn into pieces

In a large, deep cast-iron skillet, fry the bacon over moderate heat till crisp, drain on paper towels, and crumble.

Add the onion, jalapeño, and garlic to the skillet and stir till softened, about 3 minutes. Add the okra and stir for 5 minutes longer. Add the tomatoes, corn, thyme, salt and pepper, and cayenne, reduce the heat slightly, cover partially, and fry till the corn is tender, about 10 minutes, stirring from time to time. Add the basil and crumbled bacon, stir, and serve hot.

Commander's Maque Choux

MAKES 6 TO 8 SERVINGS

Not generally known outside Louisiana, maque choux is a sublime Cajun concoction, the popularity of which was revived some years ago at Commander's Palace restaurant in New Orleans. The dish is ideal with roasted or grilled meats and poultry, but when the vegetables are enhanced with shrimp, crawfish tails, or chopped cured ham, it can easily be served as an unusual and delicious main course.

½ pound bacon, cut into small pieces
1 medium onion, finely chopped
1 small green bell pepper, seeded and finely chopped
4 garlic cloves, minced
1 small hot chile pepper, seeded and minced
¼ pound small, firm, fresh okra (stems removed), cut into rounds

8 ears fresh corn, husks and silks removed, kernels cut from the cobs, and milk scraped from the cobs and reserved
¼ cup water
Salt and freshly ground black pepper to taste
4 scallions (part of green tops included), chopped
1 tablespoon butter

In a large, heavy skillet, fry the bacon over moderate heat till crisp, drain on paper towels, and reserve. Add the onion, bell pepper, garlic, and chile pepper to the skillet and fry, stirring, for about 3 minutes. Add the okra, the corn plus its milk, the water, and salt and pepper, reduce the heat to low, cover, and simmer, stirring once or twice, till the vegetables are tender, 10 to 15 minutes.

Transfer the vegetables to a serving dish, stir in the scallions and butter, and garnish the top with the bacon.

Country-Fried Vegetable Cakes

MAKES 4 TO 6 SERVINGS

These unusual fried cakes were inspired by some served with baked ham, steaks, and beef stew at an old-fashioned country restaurant in Nashville, Tennessee, and they're a nice change from standard hashed brown potatoes, boiled field peas, and baked sweet potatoes. Do feel free to experiment with other diced or shredded vegetables, as well as any variety of fresh herbs and other seasonings. The cakes should be crispy on the outside but still fairly moist within, and they are just as good warm as hot. I particularly love the cakes served with any meat, poultry, or seafood croquettes.

1 cup cooked corn kernels (fresh or frozen)
1 cup cooked black-eyed peas
1 cup finely shredded green cabbage
1 cup finely shredded carrots
1 cup diced onions
1 garlic clove, minced
1 tablespoon minced fresh thyme leaves

1 teaspoon celery salt
Freshly ground black pepper to taste
Worcestershire sauce to taste
Tabasco sauce to taste
2 large eggs, beaten
1 cup dry bread crumbs
Peanut oil for shallow frying

In a large bowl, combine the corn, peas, cabbage, carrots, onions, garlic, thyme, celery salt, pepper, Worcestershire, and Tabasco and mix with your hands till well blended. Add the eggs and bread crumbs and continue mixing till well blended and soft. Form the mixture into 12 small cakes, flatten slightly on the tops, and set aside on a platter.

In a large cast-iron skillet, heat about ¼ inch of oil over moderate heat for 2 minutes and fry the cakes in batches till golden brown and crispy on both sides, 4 to 5 minutes in all, turning once. Drain on paper towels, transfer to a heated platter, and serve hot or warm.

Grits, Rice, and Potatoes

Top-of-the-Morning Fried Grits

MAKES 4 TO 6 SERVINGS

If anything is better than buttery boiled grits on a traditional Southern breakfast of fried eggs and country ham, it is golden brown squares of grits fried quickly in lard to a crispy finish. The best grits, of course, are stone-ground if you can find them in the market or order them on the Internet, but regular or quick-cooking (not instant) grits are almost as good, and leftover chilled grits can be just as easily fried as those that are boiled from scratch as in this recipe. For a light texture, never dredge grits to be fried in cornmeal, only in flour, and remember that all grits really do need a little extra salt before being served.

---

2 cups water
2 cups milk
1 teaspoon salt, plus more to taste

1 cup regular grits
½ cup all-purpose flour
Lard for shallow frying

In a large, heavy saucepan, combine the water, milk, and salt and bring to a boil. Gradually add the grits, reduce the heat to moderate, and, stirring frequently to prevent burning, cook till the grits are thick and creamy, 20 to 25 minutes, adding a little more water if necessary.

Scrape the hot grits onto a platter to make a ¼-inch-deep layer, cover, and chill till ready to fry.

Cut the grits into squares or rectangles and dredge in the flour on both sides.

In a large cast-iron skillet, heat about ½ inch of lard over moderate heat, fry the grits till golden brown, about 2 minutes on each side, and drain briefly on paper towels. Sprinkle with extra salt, if desired, and serve hot.

Company Fried Cheese Grits

MAKES 4 TO 6 SERVINGS

Since both sour cream and cheese are added to these luscious grits before frying, the quick-cooking style not only is acceptable in flavor and texture but also requires considerably less cooking time than regular grits. The grits could be prepared for breakfast or brunch, but never are they so good as when served with fried ham steaks, quail, or fish. For the richest flavor, be sure to use only extra-sharp cheddar cheese.

---

4 cups water
1 teaspoon salt
1 cup quick-cooking grits
4 tablespoons (½ stick) butter, cut into pieces
¼ cup sour cream
1 large egg, beaten

1 cup grated extra-sharp cheddar cheese
Freshly ground black pepper to taste
Paprika to taste
½ cup all-purpose flour
Vegetable oil for shallow frying

In a large, heavy saucepan, combine the water and salt and bring to a boil. Gradually add the grits, stirring constantly, reduce the heat to moderate, and cook, stirring, till the grits are thick and creamy, about 5 minutes.

Scrape the grits into a bowl, add the butter, sour cream, egg, cheese, pepper, and paprika and stir till the mixture is well blended and smooth. Scrape the mixture into an 8-inch square pan or dish and chill till firm and ready to fry.

Cut the grits into squares or rectangles and dredge lightly in the flour.

In a large cast-iron skillet, heat about ½ inch of oil over moderate heat, fry the grits till golden brown, about 2 minutes on each side, drain briefly on paper towels, and serve hot.

Lowcountry Shrimp and Grits

MAKES 6 SERVINGS

Originating in the Carolina and Georgia Lowcountry, shrimp and grits is one of the most famous and popular Southern dishes served today in restaurants all over the country and one that exemplifies beautifully the subtle art of Southern shallow frying. On home territory, the sauce for shrimp and grits can be made with everything from bulk pork sausage to spicy andouille sausage to smoked ham, but just lately, I've been making mine simply with premium artisanal hickory- or apple-smoked bacon and find it hard to beat. Never does a grits dish call more for the superior stone-ground product than this one, so do make the effort to find some if you want your grits to be truly creamy and full flavored. And, as always, be sure to stir the grits periodically to prevent scorching.

THE SAUCE
6 slices bacon, chopped
2 small onions, chopped
1 medium green bell pepper, seeded and chopped
1 garlic clove, minced
1 teaspoon paprika
¼ teaspoon dried thyme, crumbled
¼ teaspoon dried oregano, crumbled
Salt and freshly ground black pepper to taste
1½ pounds fresh shrimp, shelled, deveined, and cut in half

1½ cups chicken broth
¼ cup heavy cream

THE GRITS
6 cups water
1½ teaspoons salt
1½ cups grits (preferably stone-ground, not instant)
3 cups half-and-half
6 tablespoons butter, cut into pieces
Freshly ground black pepper to taste

To make the sauce, fry the bacon in a large, heavy skillet over moderate heat till almost cooked, about 8 minutes. Add the onions, bell pepper, garlic, paprika, thyme, oregano, and salt and pepper and fry, stirring, till the vegetables are softened, about 5 minutes. Add the shrimp and fry, stirring, for 2 to 3 minutes. Add the broth and cook, stirring, till slightly reduced, about 5 minutes. Add the cream, return to a simmer, and cook, stirring, till the sauce is slightly thickened, 5 to 7 minutes. Remove the sauce from the heat.

To make the grits, bring the water to a rolling boil in a large, heavy saucepan, add the salt, and gradually add the grits, stirring constantly for about 5 minutes. Add the half-and-half and butter and bring to a simmer, stirring. Cover and cook the grits slowly till very smooth and creamy, stirring from time to time, 50 to 60 minutes. Season with pepper and taste for salt.

To serve, reheat the sauce till hot, spoon mounds of grits on hot serving plates, and spoon the sauce over the grits.

Fried Hominy with Bacon and Pimentos

MAKES 4 SERVINGS

Now available in cans almost everywhere, hominy is dried corn with the hull and germ removed, and when this is ground, the result is hominy grits—without question one of the great staples of the Southern kitchen. Do not confuse soft hominy, however, with ordinary grits, which are simply any unprocessed, coarsely ground dried corn, and remember that dried hominy (which I do not recommend using) must be reconstituted to produce the right moist, supple texture. Like regular cooked grits, hominy can be fried by itself for breakfast, but when other ingredients are added, as in this recipe, the dish is ideal with fried chicken, barbecued ribs, or any style of chops.

---

5 slices bacon, cut into small pieces
1 medium onion, diced
1 garlic clove, minced
One 16- to 18-ounce can hominy, drained

¼ cup diced pimentos
2 tablespoons chopped fresh parsley leaves
Salt and freshly ground black pepper to taste

In a large, heavy skillet, fry the bacon over moderate heat till browned but not crisp and drain on paper towels. Add the onion and garlic to the skillet and stir till softened, about 3 minutes. Increase the heat slightly, add the hominy, and fry till golden, about 5 minutes. Add the pimentos, parsley, drained bacon, and salt and pepper, stir for about 1 minute, and serve hot.

River Road Rice Croquettes

MAKES 4 SERVINGS

Rice has been a major crop in Louisiana and Arkansas for well over a century, and at the stately plantations that line River Road along the Mississippi from Baton Rouge to New Orleans, the number of rice dishes that come out of the large kitchens is staggering. Similar to the sweet calas of New Orleans, these savory croquettes would typically be served either at a lavish breakfast or brunch or as a side dish with roasted meats and poultry. You can also add grated cheese, ground ham, minced cooked chicken, and other herbs or spices to the batter and serve the croquettes as a main luncheon dish with a favorite salad.

1½ cups boiled, cooled rice
½ cup all-purpose flour
2 tablespoons minced onion
½ cup buttermilk
2 large eggs, beaten

½ teaspoon dried thyme, crumbled
Salt and freshly ground black pepper to taste
Tabasco sauce to taste
Peanut oil for deep frying
½ cup dry bread crumbs

In a bowl, combine the rice, flour, and onion and mix quickly till well blended but the rice still holds its shape. Add the buttermilk, eggs, thyme, salt and pepper, and Tabasco, mix till the batter is well blended, and let stand for about 25 minutes.

In a deep fryer or large cast-iron skillet, heat about 2 inches of oil to 365°F on a deep-fat thermometer.

When ready to fry, form the rice mixture into small ovals about 1½ inches in diameter and roll in the bread crumbs. Fry in the oil till golden brown, about 2 minutes, turning once with a slotted spoon, drain the croquettes on paper towels, and serve hot.

Cajun Dirty Rice

MAKES 4 TO 6 SERVINGS

Just as Savannah red rice derives its name from the tomatoes or tomato juice that color it, Cajun fried dirty rice owes its dark tint to the fried chicken gizzards and livers that make it so distinctive and delicious. Served either as a side dish or a rich, earthy main course throughout the Louisiana bayou region, dirty rice couldn't be easier to prepare, since all you do is fry the meats and vegetables, then mix them with any style of parboiled rice that's been kept hot.

---

1 pound chicken gizzards, chopped
½ pound ground pork
¼ cup vegetable oil
1 medium onion, finely chopped
1 small green bell pepper, seeded and finely chopped
1 celery rib, finely chopped
1 garlic clove, minced

2 tablespoons all-purpose flour
½ pound chicken livers, trimmed of fat and chopped
Salt and freshly ground black pepper to taste
Cayenne pepper to taste
¼ cup chicken broth
3 cups hot boiled rice

In a bowl, combine the gizzards and pork and mix till well blended.

In a large, heavy skillet, heat the oil over moderate heat, add the gizzard and pork mixture, and fry till lightly browned, about 8 minutes, stirring. Add the onion, bell pepper, celery, and garlic, sprinkle the flour over the vegetables, stir, and fry till the vegetables are softened, about 5 minutes, stirring. Add the livers, salt and pepper, and cayenne and continue frying till the livers have lost their pink color. Add the broth, return the heat to moderate, stir well, and continue cooking for about 8 minutes.

In a large bowl, combine the rice and the contents of the skillet, toss well till thoroughly blended, and serve hot.

Fried Breakfast Potatoes

MAKES 4 TO 6 SERVINGS

Potatoes will never replace grits on the traditional Southern hot breakfast plate, but when, on occasion, they stand in, it is these tangy, crunchy home fries that are the most popular. Since russet potatoes have plenty of starch and are relatively dry, they are preferable to red or white boiling potatoes for frying.

¼ cup all-purpose flour
½ teaspoon salt
¼ teaspoon freshly ground black pepper
¼ teaspoon paprika

⅛ teaspoon crushed red pepper flakes
2½ pounds (4 or 5) russet potatoes, peeled
   and cut into ¼-inch-thick slices
Vegetable oil for shallow frying

In a bowl, combine the flour, salt, pepper, paprika, and red pepper flakes and stir till well blended. Dredge the potato slices in the flour mixture, tapping off excess, and place on a plate.

In a large, heavy skillet, heat about ½ inch of oil over moderately high heat, add the potato slices, and fry till golden brown on the bottom, about 4 minutes. Turn, fry till golden brown on the other side, 3 to 4 minutes, and drain on paper towels. Serve immediately.

 To keep cooking fats as clear as possible, always shake off excess flour, breading, or batter on foods before frying.

Skillet Potato Pancakes

MAKES 4 SERVINGS

Southerners like baked, boiled, and mashed potatoes as much as anybody else, but if you really want to see Rebel eyes light up, serve these buttery, crispy, fried potato pancakes that go so well with steaks, chops, and roasts. As with any fried potatoes, starchy russets are preferable to red or white boiling potatoes, and one trick to prevent the pancakes from burning is to fry them in a mixture of both butter and oil (though personally I love my pancakes with a slightly burnt edge).

¼ cup all-purpose flour
1 large egg, beaten
1 tablespoon minced fresh chives
1 tablespoon minced fresh parsley leaves
Salt and freshly ground black pepper to taste
Cayenne pepper to taste

2½ pounds (4 or 5) russet potatoes, peeled and finely shredded
2 to 3 tablespoons heavy cream
6 tablespoons (¾ stick) butter
6 tablespoons vegetable oil

In a large bowl, combine the flour, egg, chives, parsley, salt and pepper, and cayenne and whisk steadily till there are no lumps in the mixture. Add the potatoes and stir well. Stirring, add just enough cream to form a firm but still moist batter.

In a large, heavy skillet, heat about 1 tablespoon each of the butter and oil over moderately high heat till sizzling, add 3 to 4 tablespoons of batter for each pancake, fry till golden brown and crusty, about 4 minutes on each side, and drain on paper towels. Continue frying pancakes with remaining butter, oil, and batter and serve as hot as possible.

Sweet Potato Pups

MAKES 6 SERVINGS

Southern fried sweet potatoes have been around for at least 200 years, and if you think you love ordinary French fries, wait till you taste these crispy, succulent, deep-fried pups sprinkled either with salt or brown sugar (depending on when they're served). Some cooks like to briefly parboil their strips before frying them, and while the technique does produce lighter pups, I personally think it leaches out some of the distinctive flavor. Sweet potatoes tend to bubble up more than white ones while frying, so do watch them carefully. Since fried sweet potatoes also become soggy very quickly, serve them as soon as possible.

---

2 pounds (3 or 4) sweet potatoes
Lard for deep frying

2 tablespoons bacon grease
Salt or light brown sugar to taste

With a sharp knife, peel the potatoes and slice them into strips about 2 inches long and ½ inch thick (or into ¼-inch-thick rounds). Separate the slices and allow them to air-dry for several minutes.

In a deep fryer or deep cast-iron skillet, melt about 1½ inches of lard to 365°F on a deep-fat thermometer and add the bacon grease. Plunge the potatoes into the fat in batches and, stirring frequently, fry till golden brown and crisp, 3 to 4 minutes. Drain on paper towels, sprinkle with salt or brown sugar, and serve as soon as possible.

Cajun Sticky Sweet Potatoes

MAKES 4 TO 6 SERVINGS

Louisiana sweet potatoes are surpassed in quantity and quality only by those grown in North Carolina, and when Cajuns cook any style of pig, it's almost taken for granted that sweet potatoes will be included on the menu. More often than not, the potatoes will be sliced, dredged in sugar, and quickly fried in lard or shortening till well glazed—the result of which is caramelized slices that have a sticky, delicious crunch yet are amazingly light in texture. I think the potatoes are just as good at room temperature as they are hot.

¼ cup light brown sugar
2 tablespoons granulated sugar
Salt and freshly ground black pepper to taste

1½ pounds (about 3) sweet potatoes, peeled and cut into ¼-inch-thick slices
Lard or shortening for deep frying

In a bowl, combine the two sugars and salt and pepper and stir till well blended. Lightly dredge the potato slices in the sugar mixture and place on a plate.

In a large cast-iron pot, melt about 1½ inches of lard to 365°F on a deep-fat thermometer, fry the potatoes in batches till nicely glazed and crisp, 4 to 5 minutes, turning with a slotted spoon, and drain on paper towels. Serve hot.

Breads

Farmhouse Stovetop Biscuits

MAKES ABOUT 1 DOZEN BISCUITS

The origins of these fried biscuits can no doubt be traced back to the earliest days in America, when virtually everything in a farmhouse was cooked on top of a stove to conserve as much precious heating wood as possible. Crunchy and full-flavored, the biscuits should be browned on the outside and slightly soft inside, and every effort should be made to serve them as hot as possible. The temperature of the fat is right when a morsel of dough dropped in it just begins to sizzle.

---

2 cups all-purpose flour
4 teaspoons baking powder
1 teaspoon salt

4 tablespoons chilled lard, cut into bits, plus
    4 tablespoons for shallow frying
1 cup whole milk

In a large bowl, whisk together the flour, baking powder, and salt, add the chilled lard, and rub with your fingertips till the mixture is mealy. Add the milk and mix till the dough is smooth. Pinch off 12 pieces of dough of equal size, form each piece into a ball, and flatten the balls with your hands to about ¼ inch thick.

In a medium cast-iron skillet, melt 2 tablespoons of the lard over moderate heat, add half the flattened balls, fry till both sides are browned, about 10 minutes in all, turning once, and drain on paper towels. Repeat with the remaining 2 tablespoons lard and the remaining dough balls, and serve hot.

Texas Fried Soda Biscuits

MAKES ABOUT 2 DOZEN SMALL BISCUITS

Still popular at rural cookouts throughout Texas, small, tangy fried soda biscuits have been around since the early nineteenth century, when the only leavening besides lard was a product called saleratus sold in a bright red package (the first baking soda). Early settlers had to cook most food over open fires, so biscuits were simply fried quickly in deep cast-iron pots. Fried soda biscuits are especially good with chili and any form of barbecued meats.

2½ cups all-purpose flour
2 teaspoons baking soda
1½ teaspoons salt
4 tablespoons chilled lard, cut into small pieces

1¼ cups buttermilk
Tabasco sauce to taste
Vegetable oil for deep frying

In a large bowl, whisk together the flour, baking soda, and salt, add the lard, and cut it in with a pastry cutter or rub with your fingertips till the mixture is mealy. Gradually add the buttermilk, stirring just till the dough is soft and adding the Tabasco while stirring.

Transfer the dough to a lightly floured surface, knead about 8 times, roll out about ½ inch thick, and cut out rounds with a 1½-inch biscuit cutter. Roll the scraps together and cut out more rounds.

In a large, deep cast-iron skillet, heat about 1 inch of oil to 350°F on a deep-fat thermometer, add the biscuits in batches, cover the skillet, and fry for about 3 minutes. Turn the biscuits with a slotted spoon, cover, and fry till golden and puffy, about 3 minutes longer. Drain on paper towels and serve hot or warm.

Maryland Chicken Biscuits

MAKES ABOUT 16 BISCUITS

I n Maryland, these crispy biscuits are called chicken biscuits, for the simple reason that they're traditionally shallow-fried in some of the same fat used to fry chicken—but at a higher temperature. If frying in batches, do make sure that the temperature of the oil remains at 375°F to avoid greasy biscuits, and by no means fry the biscuits for longer than 5 minutes total. When frying these biscuits, I might well add 1 or 2 tablespoons of bacon grease to the oil for wonderful additional flavor.

1½ cups all-purpose flour
3 teaspoons baking powder
¼ teaspoon baking soda
½ teaspoon salt

3 tablespoons chilled vegetable shortening
¾ cup buttermilk
Vegetable oil for shallow frying

In a bowl, whisk together the flour, baking powder, baking soda, and salt, add the shortening, and rub with your fingertips till the mixture is mealy. Gradually add the buttermilk, stirring with a wooden spoon till the dough is soft and slightly sticky.

Transfer the dough to a lightly floured surface and turn the edges toward the middle, pressing with your hands. Press the dough out about ¼ inch thick and cut straight down with a 1½-inch biscuit cutter into rounds. Gather up the scraps, press the dough out again, and cut out more rounds.

In a large cast-iron skillet, heat about 1 inch of oil to 375°F on a deep-fat thermometer, add the biscuits in batches, and fry till evenly browned, about 2 minutes on each side, turning once with a slotted spoon. Drain on paper towels and serve hot.

Hot-Water Skillet Cornbread

MAKES ABOUT 1 DOZEN CAKES

While most Southern cornbread is baked, there are some cooks who wouldn't dream of making anything other than these tender cakes quickly fried to a golden finish. For the right heat distribution, only a cast-iron skillet should be used, and remember that the batter should have the consistency of boiled grits. Serve this cornbread slathered with butter or drizzled with a little molasses.

2 cups white cornmeal
1 teaspoon salt
1 teaspoon sugar
½ teaspoon baking powder

¼ cup whole milk
1 tablespoon bacon grease
1½ cups boiling water
Vegetable oil for shallow frying

In a large bowl, combine the cornmeal, salt, sugar, and baking powder and stir till well blended. Add the milk and bacon grease and stir just till the mixture is moistened but still a little lumpy. Gradually add the boiling water, stirring constantly with a wooden spoon till the batter is the consistency of boiled grits.

In a large cast-iron skillet, heat about ½ inch of oil till very hot but not smoking and drop the batter in batches by ¼ cupfuls into the oil. Fry the cakes till golden, about 3 minutes on each side, drain on paper towels, and serve hot.

Cheddar Skillet Cornbread

MAKES 6 SERVINGS

E asy to make and particularly delicious with fried fish or shrimp, this skillet corn-bread can be lightened further by using only 1 cup of cornmeal and ½ cup of all-purpose flour. Some Southern cooks might also intensify the cheese flavor by using half grated cheddar and half grated Parmesan. I like to serve this cornbread hot directly from the skillet.

1½ cups yellow cornmeal
2 teaspoons baking powder
1 teaspoon sugar
1 teaspoon salt

1 cup milk
1 large egg
4 tablespoons (½ stick) butter, melted
1 cup grated extra-sharp cheddar cheese

In a large bowl, combine the cornmeal, baking powder, sugar, and salt and stir till well blended. In another bowl, whisk together the milk, egg, and half of the melted butter till well blended, add the cheese, and stir till well blended. Add the mixture to the dry ingredients and stir till the batter is well blended.

In a large cast-iron skillet, heat the remaining melted butter over low heat, scrape the batter into the skillet, cover, and fry slowly till the top is firm, about 20 minutes.

To serve, cut the cornbread into wedges.

Traditional Hoecakes

MAKES ABOUT 16 HOECAKES

O riginally fried on iron sheets or the metal ends of hoes over open fires by Indi-
ans and Colonial settlers, these golden, crispy cakes are also known as griddle cakes, ash cakes, or Shawnee cakes and are the earliest form of Southern
corn pone. For the best results, use a cast-iron skillet that maintains a steady heat, and
to avoid burning the cakes, make sure the heat is not too high once you begin frying.
Slathered with butter, hoecakes can be served at any meal and are also great with fruit
preserves at breakfast.

---

2 cups white cornmeal
1 teaspoon salt

1 cup boiling water
2 to 3 tablespoons bacon grease

In a bowl, combine the cornmeal and salt, then pour on the boiling water in a slow, steady
stream, beating constantly with a wooden spoon till the batter is smooth. For each hoecake, pat in
your hands about 2 tablespoons of the batter into a flat round 3 to 4 inches in diameter, and continue patting till all the batter is used up, flouring your hands if necessary.

Heat about 1 tablespoon of the bacon grease in a large cast-iron skillet over high heat, reduce
the heat to low, add a few of the hoecakes, and fry till golden brown and crisp, about 2 minutes on
each side. Repeat with the remaining grease and hoecakes, transferring them to a platter and keeping them as hot as possible till ready to serve.

Tennessee Johnnycakes

MAKES 6 SERVINGS

In Tennessee, fried griddle cakes are generally known as johnnycakes, and unlike the more primitive forms of corn pone, these are leavened not only with baking powder and egg but also with a little lard. Fry the cakes only till golden brown, and serve them either buttered with fried fish or roasted meats or fairly drenched with cane syrup or molasses for breakfast.

½ cup yellow cornmeal
½ cup all-purpose flour
1 teaspoon baking powder
1 teaspoon salt

1 tablespoon chilled lard
½ cup cold milk
1 large egg, beaten
¼ cup vegetable oil

In a bowl, combine the cornmeal, flour, baking powder, and salt and mix till well blended. Add the lard and rub with your fingertips till pea-size granules form. Stirring, gradually add the milk till the mixture is evenly moistened, add the egg, and stir till the batter is well blended and smooth.

In a large cast-iron skillet, heat the oil over moderate heat, drop the batter by rounded table-spoons into the oil, fry till golden brown, about 3 minutes on each side, and drain on paper towels. Serve the johnnycakes warm.

 Contrary to what people are led to believe, 1 tablespoon of lard contains 12 mg of cholesterol, versus 33 mg in the same quantity of butter.

Center Pier Hush Puppies

MAKES ABOUT 3 DOZEN HUSH PUPPIES

Supposedly deriving their quaint name from the efforts of early cooks to quiet yapping dogs at fish fries by tossing them scraps of bread batter and yelling "Hush, puppies!," these wonderful cornmeal dodgers are without question one of the great fried breads served at barbecues, oyster roasts, and seafood houses all over the South. Should authentic hush puppies be made with only cornmeal or a blend of cornmeal and flour? Should they contain sugar and/or onion? Must they be fried only in lard for the lightest texture? Is it a sacrilege to butter a hush puppy? All I know is that some of the most glorious pups I've eaten over a lifetime were those once served at the Center Pier restaurant at Carolina Beach, North Carolina, and that I consider myself lucky to have snagged the recipe. I also know that nothing, repeat nothing, is worse than a cold hush puppy, so take warning when serving these crispy wonders.

2 cups yellow cornmeal	2½ cups whole milk
1 cup all-purpose flour	¼ cup vegetable oil
1 tablespoon sugar	1 large egg, beaten
1 teaspoon baking powder	1 tablespoon bacon grease
1 teaspoon salt	Lard for deep frying
1 small onion, minced	

In a large bowl, combine the cornmeal, flour, sugar, baking powder, and salt and stir till well blended. Add the onion, milk, oil, egg, and bacon grease and stir with a wooden spoon just long enough to blend well.

In a deep fryer or deep cast-iron pot, heat about 3 inches of lard to 375°F on a deep-fat thermometer, drop the batter in batches by tablespoons into the fat, and fry till the hush puppies are golden brown and crisp, 3 to 4 minutes, turning as necessary. Drain briefly on paper towels and serve immediately in a covered bread basket.

Buttermilk Hush Puppies

MAKES ABOUT 3 DOZEN HUSH PUPPIES

Made with white instead of yellow cornmeal and with both buttermilk and Tabasco, these hush puppies are not only very crunchy but also delightfully tangy. Purists might frown at adding even a tablespoon of sugar, but I think it adds balance to the pups. These are the hush puppies you're likely to find at pork barbecue joints from the Carolinas to Alabama and Mississippi, and they're the ones I fry for Brunswick stew parties.

---

2 cups white cornmeal
1 cup all-purpose flour
1 tablespoon sugar
1 teaspoon baking soda
1 teaspoon salt

Freshly ground black pepper to taste
2 cups buttermilk
Tabasco sauce to taste
Vegetable oil for deep frying

In a large bowl, combine the cornmeal, flour, sugar, baking soda, salt, and pepper and stir till well blended. Make a well in the center of the mixture, add the buttermilk and Tabasco, and stir till the dry ingredients are just moistened.

In a deep fryer or deep cast-iron pot, heat about 3 inches of oil to 375°F on a deep-fat thermometer. In batches, drop the batter by rounded tablespoons into the fat, fry till golden brown and crunchy, 3 to 4 minutes, turning once, drain briefly on paper towels, and serve piping hot.

Indian Dog Bread

MAKES ABOUT 1 DOZEN CAKES

With no leavening, these crispy cornmeal cakes are probably of Indian origin and without doubt one of the earliest forms of Southern cornbread. Served with lots of butter, the cakes are ideal for dunking in the liquid ("pot likker") of boiled greens and beans and for sopping up the gravy served with roasts and fried country ham. If frying bread in pure bacon grease alarms you, substitute peanut oil flavored with only 1 or 2 tablespoons of bacon grease. In either case, heat the fat till it's quite hot but not smoking, and fry the cakes only till they are golden brown; otherwise, they will be hard.

1 cup yellow cornmeal	1 cup cold water
½ teaspoon salt	Bacon grease for shallow frying

In a bowl, combine the cornmeal and salt and gradually add the water till a fairly smooth batter forms.

In a large cast-iron skillet, heat about ½ inch of bacon grease over moderately high heat. In batches, drop the batter by rounded tablespoons into the fat and fry just till the cakes are golden brown and crisp, 2 to 3 minutes on each side, turning once. Drain on paper towels and serve hot or warm.

 Bacon grease has the same caloric value as canola, safflower, and olive oils.

Squaw Fry Bread

MAKES ABOUT 6 SERVINGS

Unlike dog bread, this updated Indian fry bread is made with flour instead of cornmeal, leavened with baking powder and a bit of shortening, and enriched with milk. Squaw bread is great with soups and stews, and I know one Southern cook who adds about ¼ cup of crumbled fried bacon to the dough and serves the bread with cane syrup at lavish breakfasts and brunches. Enhanced with a little minced onion or chives, squaw bread also goes well with fairly sophisticated luncheon chowders, hashes, and salads.

---

4 cups all-purpose flour
1 tablespoon baking powder
2 teaspoons sugar
2 teaspoons salt

1 tablespoon chilled vegetable shortening
2 cups milk
Lard or vegetable shortening for deep frying

In a bowl, combine the flour, baking powder, sugar, and salt and mix till well blended. Add the chilled shortening and work it with your fingertips till the mixture is mealy. Add the milk and beat till the dough is very soft. On a floured surface, roll out the dough about ¼ inch thick and cut it into fairly small squares.

In a large cast-iron skillet, heat about 1 inch of lard or shortening to 365°F on a deep-fat thermometer, fry the squares in batches till golden brown, 2 to 3 minutes, turning once, drain on paper towels, and serve hot or warm.

Deluxe Monte Cristo Sandwich

MAKES 1 SANDWICH

I'm not at all sure that the sumptuous Monte Cristo sandwich has origins in the South, but rest assured that only Southerners insist on dressing the interior of the sandwich with plenty of beloved mayonnaise before battering it and frying it in butter. Also, remember that a true Southern Monte Cristo is fried only till the cheese begins to melt and never till it is oozing vulgarly out the sides of the sandwich.

Mayonnaise
2 slices white loaf bread
2 slices Swiss cheese
2 thin slices cooked chicken or turkey breast
2 thin slices baked ham

¼ cup milk
1 large egg
Salt and freshly ground black pepper to taste
2 tablespoons butter

Spread mayonnaise generously on one side of each slice of bread and lay a slice of cheese on the dressed side of one bread slice. Top with the chicken and ham slices, add the other cheese slice, and top with the other bread slice, mayonnaise side down. Press the sandwich down lightly.

In a shallow dish, whisk together the milk, egg, and salt and pepper, dip the sandwich in the wash, coating the edges as well as the sides, and place on a plate, reserving any wash for another sandwich.

In a small, heavy skillet, heat 1 tablespoon of the butter over moderately low heat, add the sandwich, and fry till lightly browned on one side, about 3 minutes. Lift the sandwich with a spatula, add the remaining 1 tablespoon butter to the skillet, and fry the sandwich on the other side till browned and the cheese just begins to melt, 2 to 3 minutes. Serve warm.

Desserts

Georgia Fried Spiced Peaches

MAKES 4 SERVINGS

There's not much that Georgia cooks can't and don't do to enhance their golden Elberta and white Dixie Belle peaches, and one of the best ideas is to simply fry these legendary beauties in butter with two sugars and cinnamon, baste them with the spicy syrup, and serve them over scoops of vanilla ice cream with slices of pound cake. The only way you might improve on this recipe (as I often do) is to add a few wedges of fresh mango to the peaches—a glorious culinary marriage if ever there was one.

3 large, firm, ripe fresh peaches	3 tablespoons light brown sugar
4 tablespoons (½ stick) butter	¼ teaspoon ground cinnamon
3 tablespoons granulated sugar	Vanilla ice cream

Peel the peaches, cut them in half, remove the pits, and pat the halves dry with paper towels.

In a large enameled or stainless steel skillet, combine the butter, both sugars, and cinnamon over moderate heat and stir till the butter melts. Add the peaches cut side down and fry till the bottoms are nicely glazed, about 2 minutes. Turn them over, baste with the liquid, and fry for 2 minutes longer.

Serve the peaches over scoops of vanilla ice cream.

Dori's Skillet Dumplings and Blackberries

MAKES 4 TO 6 SERVINGS

Dori Sanders is known throughout the Carolinas not only as a peach farmer with a wildly popular farm stand near York, South Carolina, but also as an accomplished cook and cookbook author whose Southern recipes couldn't be more enticing. Over the years, Dori has come up with numerous intriguing ideas, but none is more original than these delightfully sticky fried dumplings and blackberries, which I serve warm with ice cream. Fresh blackberries, of course, are best, but partially thawed frozen ones can also be used.

1 cup all-purpose flour
1 teaspoon baking powder
½ teaspoon baking soda
½ teaspoon salt
1 cup plus 2 teaspoons sugar
⅔ cup buttermilk

1 large egg
4 tablespoons (½ stick) butter, melted
Pinch of grated nutmeg
1 quart fresh blackberries
Vanilla ice cream

In a bowl, combine the flour, baking powder, baking soda, salt, and 2 teaspoons of the sugar and mix till well blended. In another bowl, whisk together the buttermilk, egg, half of the butter, and nutmeg, add to the dry ingredients, and stir till the batter is blended but still moist.

In a large, deep skillet, heat the remaining melted butter over moderately high heat, drop the batter in batches by large tablespoons into the fat, fry till the dumplings are browned, 4 to 5 minutes per side, and drain on paper towels.

Pour the blackberries into the skillet, add the remaining 1 cup sugar, stir well, and arrange the dumplings over the berries. Reduce the heat to low, cover, and simmer for about 10 minutes.

To serve, spoon equal amounts of berries into serving bowls, top with the dumplings, and serve warm with scoops of ice cream.

Delaware Blueberry Fritters

MAKES 4 TO 6 SERVINGS

Delaware does not produce North Carolina's quantity of blueberries, but the plump lowbush variety cultivated there has exquisite flavor and texture that make the berries ideal for desserts like these beguiling fritters. Be sure to use plenty of oil for frying the fritters, and since canola is relatively bland, don't substitute a more assertive oil that might alter the dessert's overall delicate nature. While the fritters can always be served with ice cream, my friends in Delaware prefer only lots of confectioners' sugar.

---

1 cup all-purpose flour
2 teaspoons baking powder
¼ cup granulated sugar
¼ teaspoon salt
⅓ cup milk

1 large egg
Pinch of grated nutmeg
1 cup fresh blueberries
Canola oil for deep frying
Confectioners' sugar

In a bowl, combine the flour, baking powder, granulated sugar, and salt and stir till well blended. In another bowl, whisk together the milk, egg, and nutmeg till well blended, gradually add to the dry mixture, and stir till the batter is smooth. Fold in the blueberries.

In a deep fryer or Dutch oven, heat 2 to 3 inches of oil to 375°F on a deep-fat thermometer, drop ¼ cupfuls of batter in batches (3 or 4 at a time) into the oil, and fry till golden brown on one side, about 3 minutes. Turn the fritters with a slotted spoon, fry till the other sides are golden brown, about 3 minutes, and drain on paper towels.

Sprinkle the fritters generously with confectioners' sugar and serve warm.

Creole Calas

MAKES ABOUT 2 DOZEN FRITTERS

Once was the time when these hot, spongy Creole fritters were sold at stands all over the French Quarter of New Orleans, but today you almost have to be invited into a private home during Mardi Gras for the possibility of being served delectable calas at the end of a lavish meal. Although the fritters are traditionally dusted with confectioners' sugar, I think they're equally good drizzled with honey or sorghum. Calas are also delicious for breakfast.

---

2 cups boiled, cooled long-grain white rice
3 large eggs, beaten
¼ teaspoon pure vanilla extract
¼ teaspoon grated nutmeg
¼ teaspoon ground cinnamon
¼ teaspoon grated lemon rind

1 cup all-purpose flour
½ cup granulated sugar
3 teaspoons baking powder
½ teaspoon salt
1 quart peanut or canola oil
Confectioners' sugar

In a large bowl, combine the rice, eggs, vanilla, nutmeg, cinnamon, and lemon rind and stir till well blended. Into another bowl, sift together the flour, granulated sugar, baking powder, and salt, add to the rice mixture, and stir till well blended, adding a little more flour if necessary to make a batter that is thick but loose enough to be dropped easily from a spoon.

Pour the oil into a large pot and heat to about 350°F on a deep-fat thermometer. Drop the batter by heaping tablespoons into the oil, fry till nicely browned, about 3 minutes, and drain on paper towels. Dust the calas with confectioners' sugar and serve hot or warm.

 The lightest batters are made with seltzer, soda water, beer, or any other fizzy liquid.

French Market Beignets

For many, no trip to New Orleans is complete without a visit to the Café du Monde in the old French Market to eat beignets washed down with cups of strong chicory coffee, and without question these puffy doughnut-like fritters covered with confectioners' sugar are one of the most memorable fried Southern delicacies ever conceived. While the beignets are delicious by themselves, they're even more special and unusual as a dessert with crushed fresh fruit spooned over the top. Do be warned to maintain the temperature of the oil at 350°F; otherwise, the fritters could be greasy and soggy.

3 cups all-purpose flour
2 tablespoons baking powder
½ cup granulated sugar
1 teaspoon salt
1 cup whole milk

1 cup water
1 large egg
Vegetable oil for deep frying
Confectioners' sugar

In a large bowl, combine the flour, baking powder, granulated sugar, and salt and stir till well blended. In a small bowl, combine the milk, water, and egg and whisk till well blended. Add the wet ingredients to the dry ones and stir till the batter is well blended and smooth.

In a deep fryer or deep, heavy skillet, heat about 2 inches of oil to 350°F on a deep-fat thermometer. Drop the batter by heaping teaspoons into the oil about 10 at a time (never crowding the vessel), fry till puffy and golden brown on all sides, 6 to 7 minutes, turning once with a slotted spoon, and drain on paper towels. Sprinkle the beignets generously with confectioners' sugar and serve warm or at room temperature.

Bourbon Peach Turnovers

MAKES ABOUT 2 DOZEN SMALL TURNOVERS

In the South, peaches are often used to make fried dessert turnovers or small half-moon pies, but you can just as easily substitute a coarse puree of sweetened and flavored strawberries, mangoes, blueberries, or firm pears. To fully secure the edges of these turnovers for frying, one trick is to keep your fingertips moistened with water as you press the dough. Don't crowd the oil with too many turnovers at a time, and there's really no need to turn them more than once. The turnovers are best warm and crispy with maybe a spoonful of ice cream on top, but they're also delicious at room temperature.

---

2 cups all-purpose flour
1 teaspoon baking powder
½ teaspoon salt
4 tablespoons (½ stick) butter, chilled and cut into bits
4 tablespoons lard, chilled and cut into bits
6 tablespoons ice water

2 pounds ripe fresh peaches, peeled, pitted, and coarsely chopped
½ cup packed light brown sugar
¼ cup water
2 tablespoons bourbon
½ teaspoon ground cinnamon
Canola or safflower oil for deep frying
Confectioners' sugar

In a bowl, combine the flour, baking powder, and salt and stir till well blended. Add the butter and lard and rub with your fingertips till the mixture is mealy. Add the ice water and stir with a wooden spoon till the dough forms a ball. Wrap in plastic wrap and refrigerate for 1 hour before using.

In a stainless steel or enameled saucepan, combine the peaches, brown sugar, and water and bring to a boil, stirring. Reduce the heat to moderate and stir till the peaches thicken almost to a solid puree. Scrape into a bowl, add the bourbon and cinnamon, stir well, and let cool.

On a lightly floured surface, roll out the dough very thin and cut it into 4-inch rounds with a biscuit cutter. Gather up the scraps, roll out, and cut into more rounds. To shape the turnovers, spoon about 2 tablespoons of the peaches onto one half of each round, fold the other half over the peaches, and press the edges tightly to secure the filling.

In a deep fryer or large, heavy skillet, heat about 2 inches of oil to 375°F on a deep-fat thermometer and fry the turnovers in batches till golden and crisp, about 3 minutes, turning once with a slotted spoon. Drain on paper towels, sprinkle with confectioners' sugar, and serve warm or at room temperature.

Half-Moon Fried Apple Pies

MAKES 8 SERVINGS

Similar to fried fruit turnovers, spicy half-moon pies made with fresh or dried fruits are still a favorite dessert at diners and family restaurants and in rural homes all over the South, and cooks pride themselves on attaining distinctive flavors with just the right combination of spices. The pies are equally good prepared with simmered apricots, pears, or peaches, and by all means experiment with various ground spices. Do make sure that the edges of these half-moons are tightly secured before they are fried.

2 cups peeled diced cooking apples
¼ cup water
1 teaspoon fresh lemon juice
¼ cup sugar
1 tablespoon butter
¼ teaspoon ground cinnamon
⅛ teaspoon grated nutmeg

Pinch of ground cloves
2 cups all-purpose flour
1 teaspoon salt
⅔ cup chilled vegetable shortening
4 to 6 tablespoons ice water
Canola or safflower oil for deep frying

In a saucepan, combine the apples, water, lemon juice, sugar, butter, cinnamon, nutmeg, and cloves and bring to a low boil, stirring. Reduce the heat to low, cover, and cook till the apples are tender, about 15 minutes. Remove from the heat and let cool.

In a bowl, combine the flour and salt and cut in the chilled shortening till the mixture is mealy. Stirring, gradually sprinkle enough ice water over the surface just till the pastry holds together. On a floured surface, roll the pastry ⅛ inch thick and cut into eight 4-inch circles.

Place 2 tablespoons of the apples onto one half of each circle, fold the other half over the filling, and secure the edges tightly with your fingertips or a fork.

In a deep fryer or deep cast-iron skillet, heat about 2 inches of oil to 365°F on a deep-fat thermometer, fry the pies till golden brown, about 3 minutes, turning once, drain on paper towels, and serve warm.

Brown Sugar–Cinnamon Doughnut Balls

MAKES ABOUT 2½ DOZEN BALLS

Southern cooks love good doughnuts as much as anybody else and learned long ago how to make numerous homemade styles that are not only easy to produce but ten times better than most commercial ones. These spicy, crispy balls are ideal to serve with a big bowl of mixed fresh fruit, and they're also delicious with jam or sorghum at breakfast.

---

2 cups all-purpose flour
1 teaspoon baking powder
½ teaspoon baking soda
½ teaspoon salt
½ cup granulated sugar
3 tablespoons butter, melted and cooled

1 large egg
½ cup buttermilk
½ cup packed light brown sugar
1 teaspoon ground cinnamon
Canola oil for deep frying

In a medium bowl, combine the flour, baking powder, baking soda, and salt and stir till well blended. In a large bowl, combine the granulated sugar, butter, egg, and buttermilk and whisk till well blended and smooth. Add the dry ingredients to the buttermilk mixture and stir to form a soft, pliable dough. Cover the bowl with plastic wrap and refrigerate for at least 1 hour.

On a plate, mix the brown sugar and cinnamon. Using a rounded tablespoon, scoop up the chilled dough, form into balls, and place on another plate.

In a large, heavy skillet, heat about 1½ inches of oil to 350°F on a deep-fat thermometer, drop the dough balls into the oil in batches, and fry till golden brown, about 4 minutes, turning once with a slotted spoon. Drain briefly on paper towels and, while still hot, roll in the brown sugar and cinnamon mixture till well coated.

Apricot-Raisin Crepes

MAKES 6 SERVINGS

You won't find many dessert crepes in the Southern repertoire, but when I was once served these luxurious ones at a popular restaurant in Lexington, Kentucky, I didn't waste any time getting a recipe and trying to reproduce them at home. Note that the crepes can be fried in advance, rolled with the filling at the last minute, and warmed before serving. And yes, they are delicious with scoops of vanilla ice cream.

7 tablespoons butter
2 cups peeled diced fresh apricots
½ cup seedless golden raisins
½ cup granulated sugar
1 cup all-purpose flour
2 tablespoons confectioners' sugar

1 teaspoon baking powder
½ teaspoon salt
1 cup milk
2 large eggs
1 teaspoon pure vanilla extract

In a skillet, melt 3 tablespoons of the butter over moderate heat, add the apricots and raisins, and stir for 5 minutes. Sprinkle the granulated sugar over the top, stir well, cover, cook till the apricots are very soft, about 3 minutes longer, and keep the filling warm.

In a medium bowl, combine the flour, confectioners' sugar, baking powder, and salt and stir till well blended. In a small bowl, whisk together the milk, eggs, and vanilla till well blended, add to the dry ingredients, and stir till the batter is smooth.

In a small, heavy skillet, melt just enough of the remaining 4 tablespoons butter to coat the bottom of the pan, add a small amount of batter, fry till the crepe is browned on one side, about 3 minutes, turn, brown on the other side, about 3 minutes, and transfer to a plate. Repeat with the remaining butter and batter, stacking the browned crepes on the plate.

To serve, fill each crepe with about 1 tablespoon of the apricot filling, roll up, and serve warm.

Delta Pain Perdu

MAKES 4 SERVINGS

R eferring to "lost and rescued" day-old bread that is soaked or dipped in a seasoned batter, then fried till golden brown, pain perdu is the Creole version of French toast that is served either with cane syrup for breakfast or sprinkled with confectioners' sugar and topped with fresh berries for an unusual dessert. Ideally, the bread should be served as hot as possible, but if that's impractical, it's also delicious warm or even at room temperature. I do not recommend substituting slices of white loaf bread for the French bread in this recipe.

---

2 cups milk
2 large eggs
½ cup granulated sugar
½ teaspoon salt
½ teaspoon grated nutmeg
2 tablespoons brandy

1 teaspoon pure vanilla extract
8 slices day-old French bread, about 1 inch
  thick
6 tablespoons (¾ stick) butter
Confectioners' sugar
Fresh berries (optional)

In a bowl, whisk together the milk, eggs, granulated sugar, salt, nutmeg, brandy, and vanilla till well blended. Arrange the bread slices in a shallow baking pan, pour the egg mixture evenly over the tops, and let soak for about 10 minutes.

In a large, heavy skillet, melt 3 tablespoons of the butter over moderately high heat, add 4 of the bread slices, fry till browned, about 2 minutes on each side, and transfer to a heated platter. Repeat with the remaining 3 tablespoons butter and 4 bread slices.

Sprinkle the slices with confectioners' sugar, garnish with the berries, and serve immediately.

Texas Fried Cinnamon Cookies

MAKES AT LEAST 2 DOZEN COOKIES

These delightful fried cookies are the Tex-Mex version of the crisp, puffy Mexican confection known as *sopaipillas,* and although the spicy cookies are traditionally served with ice cream or fruit compotes, they also make a simple but unusual dessert when drizzled with honey or molasses. Be sure to dredge the cookies in the cinnamon mixture while they're still fairly hot.

4 cups all-purpose flour
2 teaspoons baking powder
1 teaspoon salt
½ cup chilled lard
1 cup sugar

3 large eggs, beaten
Milk
2 teaspoons ground cinnamon
Vegetable shortening for deep frying

In a bowl, combine the flour, baking powder, and salt and mix till well blended. Add the lard and work with your fingertips till the mixture is mealy. Add ½ cup of the sugar and mix till well blended. Stirring, add the eggs and just enough milk to make a firm but not stiff dough.

On a floured surface, roll out the dough ¼ inch thick and cut into 1½-inch squares. Re-roll the scraps and cut out more squares. On a plate, mix together the remaining ½ cup sugar and the cinnamon and set aside.

In a deep fryer or large skillet, heat about 1 inch of shortening to 365°F on a deep-fat thermometer and fry the squares in batches till browned, about 2 minutes on each side, turning once. Drain on paper towels, dredge the cookies in the cinnamon mixture while still hot, and let cool.

Acknowledgments

I extend my general sorghum-soaked thanks to all my nameless friends, relatives, colleagues, and cast-iron cooks scattered throughout the South who have generously shared recipes, proffered sound advice on cooking techniques and ingredients, and allowed me to pick their brains on any and every subject pertaining to the sacred Southern art of frying. In particular, a hearty salute to my expert and loyal Rebel cohorts, Jean Anderson, Fran McCullough, Kathleen Purvis, Damon Lee Fowler, Julia Reed, "Hoppin'" John Taylor, Paul Prudhomme, Louis Osteen, and Frank Stitt, and, for their enduring help and support, a big nod to Ella Brennan, James Lasyone, Mildred "Mama Dip" Council, Liz Smith, Dori Sanders, Adam Lewis, and Susan Wyler.

Thanks, finally, to my well-seasoned, devoted editor, Justin Schwartz, who has now shepherded me through five cookbooks, most with a thick Southern accent, as well as to my literary agent, Jane Dystel, for her always savvy suggestions and steadfastness.

Index

Page references in *italics* indicate photographs.